INTRODUCTION TO PSYCHOLOGY

Key To Books

EDUCATIONAL

INTRODUCTION TO PSYCHOLOGY

Exploring and understanding
human behavour

Dr Peter Marshall

Key To Books

British Library Cataloguing in Publication Data
A catalogue record of this book is available from the British Library

First published by Studymates 1999
Published by Key To Books 2011
Reprinted 2017.

Key To Books is an imprint of Oakley Books Ltd, Advantage Business Centre, 132-134 Great Ancoats Street, Manchester, M4 6DE, UK.

Note: the material contained in this book is set out in good faith for general guidance and no liability can be accepted for loss or expense incurred as a result of relying in particular circumstances on statements made in the book. The laws and regulations are complex and liable to change and readers should check the current position with the relevant authorities before making personal arrangements.

Cover design by Pentacor Design
Printed and bound in Exeter by Imprint Digital

Contents

List of illustrations

Preface

If there's one thing that bewilders psychology students more than anything else it's the lack of consensus in the literature. All tutors have heard students ask, 'How can there be several theories about the same thing? They can't all be right.' This response arises from not understanding the nature of social science knowledge.

One right explanation does not necessarily render another wrong. That's the nature of theories as opposed to laws. Simply presenting the substantive knowledge, one theory beside another, which appears to contradict it, can seem to pull the rug from under a student just when they think they've grasped the explanation.

The emphasis in this book is on understanding what is characteristic about the kinds of explanations which come from the different schools of thought. It is important to know how and why they differ and how they all share in, rather than necessarily compete in, explaining psychological behaviour.

Understand this and you will never again be stuck for a response, or contribution to any tutorial. Regardless of how much you have read up on a subject you will be able to discuss it intelligently. You will be able to reason out what, for example, a behaviourist explanation would involve, or the kind of explanation that would be given by a psychoanalyst, a psychobiologist, a humanist, or a cognitive psychologist.

The book will begin by introducing the reader to the form in which psychological knowledge is found. This will be followed by a concise coverage of the substantive areas from the viewpoints of each of the main theoretical approaches.

Peter Marshall

1

Understanding
Psychological Knowledge

One minute summary. Psychological knowledge is mainly in the form of theories. Theories can be strong or weak. Strong theories can be used for prediction. Different theories may explain the same thing at different levels of abstraction, or different instances of the same things at the same level of abstraction. The square of a correlation between two things gives the percentage of overlapping elements between them. Different approaches make different assumptions about the causes of psychological behaviour. In this chapter you will learn about:

▶ theories in psychology
▶ models in psychology
▶ the perspectives taken by different kinds of psychologists

Theories in psychology

Do you believe that phobias are caused by psychic conflicts? Do you think they are learned by association, or do you think they are learned from watching other phobic people?

Neither question can be answered in a simple yes or no fashion. I'll try to explain why. Almost all psychological knowledge exists in the form of theories.

▶ *Key definition* – A theory is an explanation which fits the facts and is supported by evidence in *some cases*.

There are virtually no direct, tidy relationships between causes and effects. The best we can hope for are statistical correlations between phenomena. The closer to 1 the correlation, the greater the proportion of cases a theory can explain. The closer to zero the smaller the proportion it can explain. Consequently, theory can be classified as *strong* or *weak*. Strong theories can be used for prediction.

Correlations

For a prediction the correlation needs to be greater than 0.7. Even that figure means that only 49% of the two things which are being correlated are one and the same thing. You take the square of the correlation to find this:

$$0.7 \times 0.7 = 0.49 = 49\% \text{ overlapping elements.}$$

If the correlation is 0.7 or less, there will be more chance that the theory will *not* explain, or predict, a particular case than that it will.

Different levels of abstraction

A second reason why we may find more than one theory to explain a particular phenomenon. It is that different theories can explain the same thing if their levels of abstraction are different.

For example, observational learning from exposure to television violence may explain aggression at a social psychological level. It does not, however, explain it at a psychobiological level. In the latter case we need to explain it in terms of physiological structures and neuro-chemicals.

Multiple causes

Thirdly, why should we expect only one condition to be capable of causing a particular kind of behaviour, or mental state? More than one thing can make a house fall down. The ground can subside, a lorry can crash into it, beetle infestation or rot can destroy its timbers, or it can collapse inwards after being gutted by fire. These things cannot be traced back to a single root cause, yet they all have the same end result. Why, then, should we expect psychological conditions to be explainable by a single, unambiguous cause?

Not only might there be different factors that can bring about the same effect, but more than one might be at work at the same time. Consequently, attending to one cause in treating a mental disorder might help, but not totally cure the illness.

Models in psychology

You will often hear psychology writers talking about **models**. These are explanations which fit the facts. There is no implication that they are the correct explanations in any of the cases, though. If there is evidence to support them, they will be classed as theories, for that is the main difference between the two. Theories are *supported by evidence*, in a proportion of cases.

▶ *Key definition* – A model is an explanation that fits the facts.

Laws and constructs

If they are supported by proof in all cases they will be classed as **laws**, but you don't get many of these in psychology. Evidence of a simple relationship between two variables is not enough for a theory, though. To be classed as a theory an explanation must contain two or more interrelated propositions supported by evidence. These simple relationships supported by evidence are known as **theoretical constructs**. You can obtain a fuller treatment of the nature of psychological knowledge and the ways in which it is generated from my book *Research Methods*, the full reference of which is provided at the end of this book.

Different perspectives in psychology

Each of the different theoretical approaches makes a different assumption about where the cause in a particular case lies, and they explain the effects logically from there. The six main theoretical approaches in psychology will be dealt with in this book. They are:

▶ behaviourist
▶ psychoanalytical
▶ cognitive
▶ psychobiological
▶ humanist
▶ social psychological.

The behaviourist approach

Behaviourists assume that psychological behaviour is learned by

conditioning, that is by making associations between behaviours and their consequences. If the consequence is rewarding the behaviour will be repeated. If it is not then it won't.

It is not always this straightforward, however. For example, people sometimes repeat a particular behaviour even though they receive condemnation, or some other punishment. This happens when individuals tend to be neglected. In such cases, condemnation is better than being ignored.

Another example is the many cases where people escape one bad personal relationship only to take up with another partner of the same type. Some people also seem to shoot themselves in the foot, metaphorically speaking. They seem to take courses of action which have failed for them before. They never seem to learn. This can be explained in terms of their being more comfortable with failure than success. They have learned how to deal with it; success would, to them, be a negative consequence.

The psychoanalytical approach

Psychoanalysts assume that mental behaviour can all be explained in terms of psychic conflicts and attempts to protect the **ego**. From the day we are born we seek to escape psychologically threatening situations. We have learned how painful is separation from those who are important to us and each time it is threatened, explicitly, or implicitly, we relive the remembered pain. We have learned that we receive their approval when we perform socially desirable behaviours and their condemnation when we do the opposite. Consequently we direct our behaviour in socially desirable ways to avoid the threat of rejection.

Sometimes our overriding motivation to please or appease others, to avoid rejection, leads us to behave in a way that is untrue to ourselves.

▶ We may say we agree with something when we do not.

▶ We may say we like something that we do not like, or that we believe something when we actually don't.

When we lie, or are untrue to ourselves, we suffer anxiety as a consequence. In addition, we fail to adapt fully to the conditions of life, for we have avoided facing up to something. Failure to adapt results in some degree of mental disorder. Sometimes the maladaption is not merely a suppression, but a repression of a feeling. This is where a thought or feeling threatens us so much that we bury it deep in our unconscious, so that we are not even aware it is there. The challenge then is not only to face up to the adaption, but to track down the hidden maladaption in the first place.

The cognitive approach

Cognitive psychologists assume that all mental behaviour can be explained in terms of thinking. Human beings are assumed to be intelligent and goal-seeking. Sometimes, however, people's thinking is faulty and so the consequences are failure or discomfort. Psychological disorders can, therefore, be remedied by discovering the faults in thinking and helping the individual to correct them.

The humanist approach

Humanist psychologists assume that human beings have free will and are self-seeking. Their main goal is self actualisation. This means matching what they are and what they think they should be, given their qualities, skills and abilities. Psychological behaviour can thus be explained in this way.

When individuals fail in this task, say the humanists, the result is mental disorder. The reason for failure is often unrealistic beliefs about what they are and what they think they ought to be in the first place. Humanist therapists try to remedy the problem by helping people be more realistic in this respect.

The social psychological approach

Social psychologists assume that psychological behaviour is socially determined. We behave as we do because others expect us to, or because we want to impress them in some way. If we are deprived of social affiliation, or it places demands upon us which are unrealistic or inconsistent with our personal beliefs or needs, symptoms of maladaption will occur.

Therapists from this school of thought see the remedies as coming from social situations. Their aims will be to help the individuals concerned to form more workable and appropriate relationships with others.

The psychobiological approach

Psychobiologists assume that psychological behaviour is due to biological factors. When things go wrong they assume the remedies lie in changing the physiological conditions. This can involve manipulating or modifying the physiological structures. Alternatively, it can mean controlling, increasing, reducing, or augmenting the brain chemical actions thought to be involved in the disordered behaviour.

Tutorial

Cognitive psychology focuses upon:

▶ psychic conflicts ☐
▶ social relations ☐
▶ thinking processes ☐

Tick the appropriate box.

Humanist psychologists, cognitive psychologists and social psychologists all differ in their:

▶ methods ☐
▶ basic assumptions ☐
▶ interests ☐

Tick the appropriate box.

Progress questions

How useful are each of the psychological perspectives? How might you judge their usefulness?

Seminar discussion

Take some aspect of your own, regular behaviour – your accent, your manner of speaking, your level of motivation, your beliefs about yourself, your achievement level, your interests, your habits, your moral principles, or your attitudes, for example. Consider the influences which underlie them. How much are they due to the examples you have been set, to the rewards and punishments you have received, to your thinking style, and to your desire to 'fit in' socially?

2

Attention

One minute summary – Attention theorists study which things we attend to, to what degree, and for how long we attend to them. There are single channel, dynamic, and modular models of attention. Single channel models differ over the position of the filter. Dynamic models refute a single channel process. The modular view is that there is not one process, but different mechanisms for different tasks. Attention can be seen as, to some degree, a skill. The main influences on attentional performance are *task similarity*, *difficulty* and *practice*.

By the time you have finished this chapter you should, ideally

▶ know what contributions to understanding *attention* are made by each of the main schools of thought. You should, thus, be able to tackle questions on *attention* from the following perspectives:

behaviourist	cognitive
humanist	psychoanalytical
psychobiological	social psychology

▶ know all the main theories and models of attention

▶ have developed an enhanced understanding of how attention can benefit you in your life, and the society in which you live.

Like perception, **attention** is a state in which the mind is taking in data. The essential difference between attention and perception, however, is intention. When you are perceiving something you may not necessarily be aware you are doing so. With attention, however, the action is voluntary and conscious.[1]

▶ *Key definition* – Attention is focused consciousness.

Attention theorists study:

1. the number of things people can attend to at once
2. how long people can focus attention
3. how vigilant people are
4. how people select what to attend to.

Single channel models

Single channel models explain the process of attention in terms of only one thing being processed at a time. This necessitates some kind of filter mechanism to select out what is to be attended to from what is not.

There are a number of single channel models. The main difference between them is the location of the filter, that is whether it has its effect close to the start of the process, close to the end of it, or somewhere in between.[2,4,5&6]

Broadbent's filter model

One of the earliest models was constructed by Broadbent.[2] This proposed that the filter is at the start of the process. This model provides that our sensory organs represent single channels.

There are weaknesses to this model, though. How often have you been listening to somebody in conversation when suddenly you hear your name mentioned by somebody else? If your ears could attend to only one thing at a time, this could not happen. This has become known as the **cocktail party effect**.[3]

Sensory data which your mind is processing, even though you are focusing on something else, are known as **shadowed messages**. That such processing does take place is now pretty well established.[3,8 & 13]

The degree to which a person will attend to a shadowed message is influenced by their semantic and grammatical skills.

Treisman's attenuator model

Treisman[4] constructed a model which overcame the weaknesses of

Broadbent's model. He proposed that rather than untargeted data being blocked out it was merely turned down. It remained available, therefore, but at a lower and less intrusive amplitude.[4]

The pertinence model
The pertinence model, constructed by Deutsch and Deutsch,[5] suggests that all data are processed to some degree.

According to this model, the attentional process assesses the relative importance of processing various kinds of data reaching our sensory organs and in this way determines the focus. This model has been heavily challenged.[7,9,18,19,20]

The dynamic view of attention

Many psychologists now believe that the attentional process is more complex than any single channel model can provide for. Kahneman, like Broadbent, believes that the processing capacity of the human brain is limited. However, he proposes that it handles the problem by means of a **central allocation policy**. This allocates attentional resources on the basis of the nature of the incoming data, the individual's own intention, the state of arousal, and the aggregate level of demand on the system at the time.[20]

Baddeley and Hitch's two system model
Baddeley and Hitch constructed a still more refined model. They proposed that two separate systems exist for sequential and spatial processing. These, they referred to as an **articulatory loop** and a **visuo-spatial scratch pad.** They operate under the control of a **central processor**. The latter is modality free, that is it is not specific to any of the senses in particular. Whilst the central processor functions intelligently, the two mechanisms that it controls function largely automatically.[10,11&21]

The modular view

Some psychologists prefer to think of attention, not as one process for all data and all purposes, but different mechanisms for different tasks. When attentional tasks compete for the same kinds of attentional resources, confusion occurs.[12&14]

It is plausible that training and practice can improve attentional performance. There are many areas in life where this is evident, for example fighter pilot training, and racing car training. Indeed, Neisser argues that attention should be conceptualised as a skill rather than a process.[7]

Influences on attentional performance

The main influences on attentional performance are as follows:

▶ task similarity
▶ difficulty
▶ practice.[13]

The most important task similarities are as follows:

▶ stimulus modality
▶ processing stage
▶ memory codes.[14]

The difficulty of a task is not simply the sum of the difficulty of all its sub-tasks. It's more than that. There are problems of interference to contend with as the elements of a complex task compete for attentional resources.

In addition, such sub-tasks are not performed in isolation, but have to be combined and co-ordinated. These problems make additional demands on attentional resources.[13]

Why practice works

The main reasons why practice improves attentional performance are as follows:

▶ Methods of contending with interference (from other sub-tasks and from extraneous sources) develop over time.

▶ Demands of attentional resources decrease as processing becomes more automatic.

▶ Methods of operation may be streamlined and tweaked to greater efficiency.[13]

Logan proposes an explanation in terms of a progression towards automaticity of actions. Every time we repeat an action our memory trace becomes more detailed. When all the information needed to perform an action is accessibly stored within the memory trace, no decisions and, therefore, no thought is necessary.[15]

Automaticity
Actions can be:

1. consciously controlled
2. partially automatic
3. fully automatic.[16&17]

Qualities of automatic actions
The qualities of our automatic actions are as follows:

1. they are fast
2. they do not make demands on attention
3. they are performed unconsciously
4. they are unavoidable.[13]

Tutorial

Practice questions
1. Which approach does Baddeley and Hitch's two system model represent? Tick the appropriate box.

Behaviourist	☐
Cognitive	☐
Psychoanalytical	☐
Psychobiological	☐
Humanist	☐
Social psychological	☐

2. Try to list as many of the models of attention as you can, without referring back.

3. What are the three main influences on attentional performance?

4. What are the three principle elements of Baddeley and Hitch's model?

5. How does Logan explain automaticity?

6. Why does practice improve attention?

Seminar discussion
Consider the different kinds of demands that various occupational roles place on the attention mechanism. Take the following occupations, for example:

► sports commentator
► news broadcaster
► house-husband/wife
► shop assistant
► racing driver
► scientist.

Revision, course work and exam tips
To get the maximum benefit from classes and lectures you need to prepare for them in advance. Prepare a list of questions to ask and opinions to express. Where lectures are concerned, prepare a list of questions to which you hope the lecturer will provide answers.

Get involved in any group work you are set. Don't sit on the sidelines. Be assertive, but not aggressive in expressing your opinions.

Bibliographical notes
[1]   See James 1890
[2]   Broadbent 1958
[3]   Cherry 1953
[4]   Treisman 1964
[5]   Deutsch and Deutsch 1963
[6]   Norman 1976
[7]   Neisser 1976
[8]   Allport et al. 1972
[9]   Eysenck 1984
[10] Baddeley and Hitch 1974
[11] Baddeley 1986
[12] Allport 1980
[13] Eysenck and Keane 1995
[14] Wickens 1984
[15] Logan 1988
[16] Norman and Shallice 1980
[17] Shallice 1982
[18] Solso 1979
[19] Treisman and Geffen 1967
[20] Kahneman 1973
[21] Baddeley 1996

3

Perception

One minute summary – At least some aspects of perception appear to be learned. Perception is affected by perceptual defence. The two main approaches to perception are known as bottom up and top down approaches. It is reasonable to assume it is a bit of both. Bottom up approaches cannot explain illusions. There are three main approaches to pattern recognition: feature detection, prototypes and template matching. The perceptual set is the selection of things to attend to.

When you have finished this chapter you should know what contributions to understanding of perception are made by each of the main schools of thought. You should, thus, be able to tackle questions on perception from the following perspectives:

▶ behaviourist   ▶ cognitive
▶ humanist   ▶ psychoanalytical
▶ psychobiological   ▶ social psychology

You should know all the main theories and models of perception.

The last chapter dealt with focused consciousness, *i.e.* attention. This chapter deals with how we comprehend what we are attending to.

Perspectives

It is largely the **cognitive** perspective that features in research into perception, but other schools of thought contribute, too. Here are some examples:

behaviourist	learned perceptual skills, such as picture perception[1]
psychoanalysis	perceptual defence
psychobiology	the physiology of perception
social	cultural influences on perceptual set
gestalt	the holistic nature of perception.

Some aspects of perception which psychologists focus on are:

▶ whether it starts from what is 'out there', or from what is in the head
▶ whether it is innate or learned
▶ perception of depth
▶ perception of movement
▶ perceptual constancy
▶ perceptual set
▶ perceptual defence
▶ illusions
▶ pattern recognition.

Sources of research data
Sources of research data used in the study of perception include:

1. new born babies
2. animals
3. illusions
4. cross cultural studies.

Defining perception

Before looking at the various approaches to the understanding of perception, let us first look at two different ways it has been defined.

▶ Coon defines perception as follows: '...the process of assembling sensations into a useable mental representation of the world.'[1]

▶ Gregory defines it like this: '...a dynamic searching for the best interpretation of the available data... Perception involves going beyond the immediately given evidence of the senses.'[2&8]

The difference between these two is that one sees perception as building up a complex mental image from the parts. The second one takes as the starting point the internal concept and screens external data to find the best match. Direction of flow is more or less opposite in the two models.

The divergence in the knowledge

It is along these two lines of divergence which models and theories of perception have developed. They are referred to as **bottom up** and **top down** approaches. Three approaches can be identified:

1. bottom up approaches
2. top down approaches
3. combination approaches

The nature/nurture controversy

Like other areas of psychology, the study of perception is subject to differences of belief as to whether nature or nurture is the main source. Examples of arguments from each viewpoint are as follows:

▶ *nature* – Complex perceptual abilities manifest themselves in early infancy too early to have been learned.[3]

▶ *nurture* – People of some primitive cultures cannot perceive pictures as images of reality. They cannot, for example, see depth in them.[4]

Bottom up approaches

Bottom up approaches start with the actual, concrete reality being perceived. In the case of visual perception this amounts to a pattern of light.

Studying Psychology

Gibson's direct perception theory

One of the most prominent of the bottom up theories is Gibson's Direct Perception Theory.[7] To Gibson, perception is simply the inflow of data from the external world. All the information necessary for us to comprehend and interact with our environment is out there and available to our senses. There are several types of such information:

optic flow patterns
texture gradients
linear perspective
motion parallax
context
superimposition.

Optic flow patterns

Optic flow patterns refer to the way visual features of our environment appear to behave when we are moving. The centre of our focus appears to stand still. The features all around that point, however, appear to move past us, to our sides, over our heads and beneath us, at speeds decreasing as they extend outwards from the centre.

Texture gradients

Differences in texture gradients give us information about how far away from us things are. The surface of bricks, for example, will look rougher close up than they will far away. Trees in the distance tend to look smooth, as if they were painted on canvas, rather than rugged and textured, as they would appear close up.

Linear perspective

Other things which give us information about distance include linear perspective. This is the way that parallel lines appear to converge as they get further away. Looking down a long, straight road, it will appear narrower in the distance than it does where you are standing.

Motion parallax

Motion parallax is another thing that gives us information about relative distance in a visual scene. It refers to the way the more distant an object the more slow its relative speed appears to be. When a train is moving at 100 mph the houses near the track will appear to be moving the other way at a very fast rate. The houses in the distance, however, will appear to move the other way more slowly.

Context
The further away from us objects are, the smaller and the closer to the horizon they appear to be.

Superimposition
Superimposition is a powerful source of data on relative distance, or depth in a scene. If a tree obscures the front of a house, it tells us it is closer than the house.

Top down approaches

The major theorist among top down approaches is Gregory. He argued that perception is a process of formulating and testing hypotheses.[6]

We make inferences about what is 'out there' and the actual sensory data we take in confirm, or challenge them. If the sensory data does not confirm the hypothesis, we reject it. There are many rules we apply to make the inferences. They include:

size constancy
shape constancy
colour constancy
brightness constancy
localisation constancy

▶ *Example* – People in the distance appear smaller than those in the foreground. If we did not use a rule to make an adjustment to what appears to our retina, we would assume that all people in close proximity to us are actually larger than those far away. We know this is not true so we use a rule which gives our perception the quality of **size constancy,** in other words we make allowances for the effect of distance.

Other kinds of constancy of perception prevail in the face of data to the contrary. For example, grass and trees in the distance have a bluish tinge and the further into the distance they recede the bluer they are. We don't perceive them as blue, though. We make allowances.

We also make adjustments where ovals appear when we know the actual objects are round. An example is the rim of a cup seen on a slant. These rules for making adjustments come from:

► expectations
► habit
► inference
► memory.

Illusions

We all know that illusions exist. Gibson's theories cannot explain them, for if perception were simply derived from the sensory data, it would mean impossible things exist out there in the world. Gregory's theory can account for them, though – they are hypotheses not confirmed by sensory data.[6]

Four types of illusion can be distinguished:

1. ambiguous figures
2. distortions
3. fictions
4. paradoxical figures

Many fall into more than one category.

Weaknesses of Gregory's model

The weaknesses of Gregory's model are as follows:

► Illusions persist despite awareness of their falsity.
► If the process is concept led, what starts it off?[18]
► How is it that we all tend to make the same kinds of perceptions?[18]

Combination approaches

Could it be that both 'bottom up' and 'top down' approaches apply?

It has, indeed, been argued so. Eysenck and Keane propose that 'bottom up' approaches are used when viewing conditions are good and 'top down' approaches when they are not.[19]

Neisser's (1976) Analysis By Synthesis Model

The most well worked out model of a combination approach is, perhaps, Neisser's **Analysis By Synthesis Model**.[22] Here perception is a cyclical process. Hypotheses formulated in the mind lead to the search for relevant data to confirm them. This leads to additional data which has not been deliberately sought out and this has to be analysed. This may lead to modification of the hypothesis and so the cycle goes on.

Pattern recognition

Putting aside the issue of whether the process flows from the sensory data to the mind, vice versa, or both, let us consider *how* we recognise objects for what they are. There are three major theories:

1. feature detection
2. prototypes
3. template matching

Feature detection

Feature detection theories propose that objects comprise a number of basic features, including:

► points
► straight lines
► curves.

Simple, complex and hyper-complex cortical cells have been identified which, it is thought, may be **feature detectors.**[25]

There are challenges to the feature detection approach. For one thing feature detection is essentially a **serial process,**[26] yet it is known that visual processing involves a considerable amount of **parallel processing.**

Prototypes

Prototype explanations of pattern recognition assume that we store prototypical elements of a pattern and we recognise these and combine them to perceive the full pattern.[26]

Biederman's *Recognition by Components Model* suggests that we hold 24 primitive shapes. He refers to these as **geons**, a term derived from the idea of geometrical ions. From these we construct and recognise more complex shapes.[27]

Template matching

The **template-matching hypothesis** suggests that everything we have experienced in the past becomes a template for matching objects and situations in the future. The problem is that, for this to be true, we would have to store so many templates we would have no room left in our brains.[28]

Marr set out to explain the entire process of perception, from the intake of light upon the retina to the meaningful comprehension of the scene in the mind. He argued that it is necessary to study three levels of processing:

1. tasks and methods
2. sub-processes and representations involved
3. neurological processes.[29]

To Marr the primary purpose of seeing is to determine the shape of an object. His studies led him to conclude that there are 4 stages to this:

(a) capturing the image on the retina
(b) identification of boundaries and configuration of sub-parts in the overall shape
(c) identification of direct clues to depth in the shape
(d) comprehension as a 3 dimensional object, including inferring what is not in view.

Perceptual set

We do not perceive everything that presents itself to our senses. If we did our system would overload and we would simply be confused by it all. We select out certain features to perceive and these are the elements of our **perceptual set**.[30]

Perceptual set is not only a selector, but an interpreter too. It determines the way we will interpret things that present themselves to our senses.[31]

The precise nature of an individual's perceptual set is determined by a range of factors:

> context
> culture
> expense, or object value
> expectations based on experience
> emotions
> personality
> instructions
> training/learning
> motivation
> reward and punishment.

▶ *Example* 1 – If you are hungry you will be likely to spot food around you; if you are not you may well overlook it.

▶ *Example* 2 – A customs officer is likely to notice things which indicate that someone might be smuggling, while the rest of us would miss such signs. This is because the officer's perceptual set has been trained to pick up such things.

Punishment and reward

Punishment and reward affect the perceptual set, too. The more you have gained from noticing certain things, the more you are likely to notice them. Conversely, the more you have suffered from noticing things, the less you are likely to see them.

If you have usually found approving looks whenever you have watched people's reactions to you, you will be more likely to include peoples facial expressions in your perceptual set. In contrast, if people usually respond with disapproving looks, you are less likely to focus upon this aspect of situations.

Past experience

Past experience plays a part in determining perceptual set and, in turn, the interpretation of sensory data.

This is the way Gregory[2] explains the Müller Lyer Illusion (Figure 1). He points out that the shape which has inward sloping fins suggests an external corner of a building, where the walls are receding away from us (linear perspective effect). Here, the upright corner is nearer to us than the walls. The shape with the outward sloping fins suggests an internal corner of the room, with the walls to each side extending towards us. The corner is the furthest part in the image. We would expect an upright line far away to appear shorter than an equal upright line close to us.

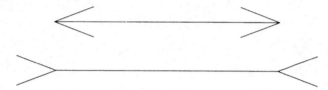

Figure 1. The Müller Lyer illusion.

Perceptual accentuation

The effect of talking to someone about a difficult area in a particular issue for decision is known as **perceptual accentuation,** or **perceptual sensitisation.** It affects the decision maker's perceptual set in two ways:

▶ by influencing the features they will select for attention
▶ by influencing the way they will interpret them.

Perceptual defence

There is also a phenomenon known as perceptual defence. An individual's perceptual set seems to serve to protect the individual from the effects of negative emotional connotations of sensory data.[35]

Taboo words

Evidence that the perceptual set works to protect the ego has come from research which has presented subjects with *neutral* and *taboo* words, including vulgar terms. It was found that taboo words were recalled more slowly and with less accuracy than neutral words.[33,35]

It may not have been the recall which was problematic, though, but the admission, or verbalisation of it. The individuals may simply have been embarrassed about saying vulgar words.[36]

If our perceptual set enables us to defend ourselves against sensory data which will be threatening, though, how can it know it will be threatening before it has perceived it?[26]

Subception

The idea of subception has been put forward as an answer to this. This is identification as threatening by the autonomic nervous system, which controls emotional reactions, prior to perception. It is sometimes known as subliminal perception, blind sight, or just a feeling.[37]

Summary

▶ At least some aspects of perception appear to be learned.

▶ Perception is affected by **perceptual defence.**

▶ The two main approaches to perception are known as **bottom up** and **top down** approaches. It is reasonable to assume it is a bit of both.

▶ Bottom up approaches cannot explain illusions.

▶ There are three main approaches to pattern recognition: **feature detection, prototypes** and **template matching.**

▶ The perceptual set is the selection of things to attend to.

Tutorial

Practice questions

1. 'Gibson's model is an example of a: bottom up/top down/ combination approach'. Delete as applicable.

2. List as many models of perception as you can.

3. What are bottom up, top down and combination approaches?

4. What are:
> optic flow patterns
> texture gradients
> linear perspective
> motion parallax
> superimposition?

5. What are the following:
> size constancy
> shape constancy
> colour constancy
> brightness constancy
> localisation constancy?

6. Name three major theories of pattern recognition.

Seminar discussion
To what extent do people see what suits them?

Coursework, revision and exam tips
Don't be an amateur in the library. Attend the library seminar to learn how to use it effectively, or ask the library staff. Merely browsing wastes a great deal of time.

Bibliographical notes

[1] Coon 1993
[2] Gregory 1966
[3] Bower 1977
[4] Deregowksi 1972
[5] Gibson 1950
[6] Gregory 1983
[7] Gibson 1979
[8] Gregory 1966
[9] Rubin 1915
[10] Necker 1832
[11] Müller Lyer 1889
[12] Ficke 1851
[13] Ponzo 1913
[14] Zöllner 1860
[15] Wundt 1898
[16] Kanisza triangle
[17] Penrose impossible triangle
[18] Gordon 1989
[19] Eysenck and Keane 1990
[20] Brunswick 1956
[21] Eysenck and Keane 1995
[22] Neisser 1976
[23] Neisser 1964
[24] Rabbitt 1967
[25] Hubel and Wiesel 1968
[26] Eysenck 1984
[27] Biederman 1987
[28] Solso 1995
[29] Marr 1982
[30] Allport 1955
[31] Vernon 1955
[32] Minturn and Bruner 1951
[33] Bruner and Postman 1949
[34] Gregory 1983
[35] McGinnies 1949
[36] Howes and Solomon 1950
[37] Weiskrantz 1986

4

Memory

One minute summary – The main divergence in the knowledge on memory is between theories that assume a dual nature of memory (long- and short-term) and theories that refute this. Long-term memory lasts for a long time, perhaps for life. Short-term memory lasts for only a short time – 15-30 seconds. Level of processing theory holds that there are not two different kinds of memory but just one. It is the depth of processing that determines how long the memory will last. Procedural memory works by conditioning. Declarative memory works by conscious learning. Psychoanalysts are more concerned with *forgetting*, which appears to be quite a different process from storage. Reconstructive memory is *memory* plus *guess work and calculation*. It is, thus, prone to inaccuracy.

By the time you have finished this chapter you should know what contributions to the understanding of memory are made by each of the main schools of thought. You should then be able to:

▶ tackle questions on memory from the following perspectives:

behaviourist	psychoanalytical
cognitive	psychobiological
humanist	social psychology.

▶ You should know all about the main theories and models of memory.

▶ You will gain an understanding of how enhanced understanding of memory can help you make the most of your life and how it can help the society in which you live develop to the benefit of all.

Long-term and short-term memory

The most fundamental divergence in the literature on memory is whether long-term memory and short-term memory are different things.

Atkinson and Shiffrin

The view that long-term memory and short-term memory are different processes is embodied in Atkinson and Shiffrin's model.[1] It provides that information comes in to the short-term memory via the sensory organs. If it is processed in some way it is transferred to long-term memory, where it can remain for life, otherwise it is lost from short-term memory within 15–30 seconds.

Craik and Lockhart

The alternative view is embodied in Craik and Lockhart's[2] level of processing model. This provides that, rather than two separate stores, there is only one. It is the depth to which the information is processed which determines whether it will remain or not. The more information is processed the stronger the memory trace will be and, therefore, the more enduring the memory.

Long-term memory

Three things which cognitive psychologists are interested in are: the content and structure of long-term memory, the codes it uses, and how we can make the best of it.

Content and structure

This section will deal with:

▶ the form in which long-term memory appears to hold data
▶ the categories of data it appears to hold
▶ the structure of long-term memory.

Schemata theory

Schemata is the plural of schema (see page 78). Schemata are configurations of permanently modified neural pathways as a result of experience. They are mappings of experience of interaction with the external world onto the cerebrum. As a result of them an individual can relive, or recall, an experience after it has happened.

Schemata become interconnected so that we can make connections between different facts.

Slots
Schemata have slots in which we can change one bit of data for another.[5] We can, for example, put ourselves in the place of someone else in a particular stored event. This enables us to make predictions about the consequences of behaving in a particular way.

We have schemata representing various levels of abstraction,[5] for example:

▶ family
▶ local community
▶ society.[4,5,6,8,9,11]

Two relatively separate parts of long-term memory have been identified:

1. episodic memory (EM)
2. semantic memory (SM).[10]

Episodic memory
Episodic memory appears to hold autobiographical data, including:

> time
> place
> experience.[10]

Semantic memory
Semantic memory contains such things as:

> concepts
> facts
> language
> rules
> words.[10]

Semantic memory is, inevitably, more structured than episodic memory and, therefore, it is more stable and retrievable. In the latter, we tend to simply take and store experience as it comes to us in its rather random fashion.

Structure of semantic memory

Semantic memory is believed to be non-hierarchical.[21] Distance between stored concepts represents how readily associations will be made with other concepts and a variety of different kinds of link were included between concepts. The kinds of link found between concepts include:

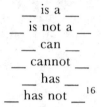

    __ is a __
   __ is not a __
     __ can __
   __ cannot __
    __ has __
  __ has not __ [16]

Weaknesses of the level of processing model

(a) It is too simple.[17]

(b) There is evidence to suggest that minimum, but meaningful elaboration can be more effective than multiple, but less meaningful elaboration.[18]

(c) The difficulty in measuring the depth to which data has been processed.[9]

Codes and cues

Long-term memory appears to employ semantic coding, but also acoustic and visual codes and, perhaps, even others.

Cued recall is recall aided by forms of cues encoded with the data. These amount to other data intentionally, or unintentionally, stored at the same time. Cues can be:

▶ internal (for example, state of mind)
▶ external (for example, context).

If you store material in a particular context, you may recall it better in the same context than in a different one. Differences of context can reduce recall potential by as much as 30%.[22]

Context is only important in situations where recall is required.[24] Where recognition of material is called for, as in multiple choice questions, context does not seem to have a significant effect.

Mood congruency

When your conditions of life are positive and everything is going well you will feel happy. Consequently, in the future, when you feel happy you will remember the things that went well for you in the past. Conversely, when times are difficult, you are likely to be unhappy. In the future, when you are unhappy, you will be more likely to remember the bad experiences. This is because the bad feelings were stored along with the bad memories just as the good feelings were stored along with good memories.[25]

Short-term memory

Short-term memory is sometimes referred to as working memory, because it holds data while it is being processed. It is believed to have four components:

1. central executive
2. articulatory loop
3. visuo-spatial scratchpad
4. primary acoustic store.

The articulatory loop is a sort of inner voice, a verbal rehearsal mechanism for auditory information. It is active when we repeat phone numbers to ourselves, for example.

The primary acoustic store[20] has a limited capacity for storing auditory information. Information reaches it directly, through the ears, from the original source (for example a person speaking to us) or from the echo in the articulatory loop, sited in the inner ear.

The visuo-spatial scratchpad does not have a primary store to transfer information to. Instead, visual information has to be converted to phonological code and, thus, fed to the primary acoustic store via the articulatory loop.[26]

The central executive controls the allocation of resources to each part of the mechanism.[26] It is modality free, so different kinds of sensory data can be dealt with simultaneously.

The articulatory loop and visuo-spatial scratchpad are not modality free and, because of this, subsequent data of the same modality will displace data present in either of these parts.

Recent models

Paivio posited a short-term memory mechanism which involved a verbal and a non-verbal component.[15] The verbal component converted data into signals which he referred to as **logogens** and the non-verbal converted visual data into **imagens**. Referential links are made between each component. The imagens of the visual data connect with verbal counterparts in the verbal component, and vice versa.

Memory types

- ▶ autobiographical, episodic memory (involving passive storage of experience)[6]
- ▶ experimental, episodic memory (involving deliberate storage of data)[6]
- ▶ declarative memory (knowledge store)[16]
- ▶ procedural memory (skill store)[14]
- ▶ echoic memory (acoustic store of very short duration)[24]
- ▶ eidetic memory (where emotional charge imprints data strongly in memory)
- ▶ long-term memory (long-term storage)[1]
- ▶ short-term memory (working memory)[12]
- ▶ iconic memory (memory form lasting only about half a second)[24]
- ▶ semantic memory[10]
- ▶ reconstructive memory (mixture of true and unwittingly made up memories)[8]
- ▶ cue dependent memory (recalled dependent on cue)
- ▶ context dependent memory (recall dependent on setting)
- ▶ state dependent memory (recall dependent on state of mind)
- ▶ flashbulb memory[13]
- ▶ prospective memory.[25]

Reconstructive memory

Autobiographical memory is particularly prone to error. This has important implications. Firstly, eyewitness testimony in legal cases cannot be taken at face value.[23,28] In addition, some well publicised child abuse cases in the last decade were both founded on and defeated by the quality of reconstructive memory.

The problem of interpretation

The main problem with reconstructive memory is that it is subject to a double level of interpretation. First, people interpret experiences at the time they occur, making deletions and distortions as necessary to make them comprehensible and consistent. Then, sometime later, when parts of the experience have become inaccessible due to various sources of forgetting, the gaps are filled in with whatever material is available – for example bits of dreams (daydreams and night dreams), material from stories, and rumours.

Furthermore, when we recall an event, we are to some degree reliving it. When we first experienced the event we made deletions and distortions, for without deleting the majority of features our perception would have overloaded. We only attend to a fraction of all the data present. When we recall or reconstruct it we make further deletions and distortions to make the data consistent with our current thinking. If several years have passed since the event, our current thinking patterns and quality of schemata will have changed, so our interpretation will be different this time.

Confabulation

Even more serious is the process of **confabulation.** When individuals are in a state of extreme emotional arousal they tend to make up information which will make their account of events coherent, consistent and logical. This is not exactly culpable lying, for at the time they may not be very aware of the falsity of their statements. Sufferers of Korsakoff's syndrome, a brain deterioration condition resulting from extreme alcohol abuse, are particularly prone to this.

Forgetting

There are various reasons why we forget things. These include:

▶ trace decay
▶ retroactive interference
▶ proactive interference

▶ displacement
▶ motivated forgetting of various types.

Displacement
Displacement affects short-term memory. New features attended to will displace data already there. Remember that visual data ends up as verbal data, as this is the only kind of data short-term memory appears to be able to store.[13,21,22]

Prevention of consolidation
A major cause of forgetting material transferred to long-term memory is failure of the consolidation process. After material has been transferred to long-term memory, a period of time for consolidation, to fix it, is required. An hour appears to be adequate.[29]

Internal and external sources of interference
Interference can come from:

> Internal sources – material already stored in memory
> External sources – data present in one's perceptual set.

It has been argued that internal sources are probably the most powerful.

Retroactive and proactive interference
Interference can affect

> what is presently stored – retroactive interference
> what is yet to be stored – proactive interference.

▶ *Retroactive interference* – is where memory is obscured, or polluted by data stored subsequently.

▶ *Proactive interference* – is where memories are obscured or polluted by material stored earlier. It appears to increase with time.[30] This is understandable, since the amount of material stored and available as a source of interference also grows over time.

Eyewitness testimony

Retroactive interference has important consequences for eyewitness testimony in court proceedings. It has been argued that the form of questions used can influence the witnesses in their reconstruction of events. For example, using 'the' instead of 'a' can lead the witness to interpret things more positively, though this may mean less accurately.

The choice of action verbs is another example. Asking somebody what speed a car was doing when it *bumped* another car is likely to elicit a different response (slower speed) than if you asked them what speed it was doing when it *crashed* into the other car.[28]

Words used are likely to have greater effect where:

▶ the witness is not expecting to be misled
▶ there has been a significant lapse of time since the event.[31]

Taking a psychobiological approach

There are biological aspects to the memory process – the physiological structures involved, and the sources of retention and erosion, particularly when the latter is due to brain damage.

The physiological components of memory

A number of structures of the brain have been identified as playing a part in memory. These parts comprise a circuit which connects the temporal and frontal lobes of the brain, and parts of the limbic system, namely the hippocampus and mamillary bodies.[25]

Short-term memory

A short-term memory trace is a product of mutual excitation among a group of neurons.[33]

Long-term memory

The actual physiological process believed to be involved in long-term memory is known as long-term potentiation (LTP). This involves high frequency stimulation of the pre-synaptic mechanism, which causes the neuron to release glutamate. A substance known as NMDA plays an important role in bringing long-term potentiation about.[32]

Synesthesia

Synesthesia is the crossing of senses. Some people see particular colours when they hear particular sounds, for example. Where such conditions are present processing will be multi-layered and, thus, strengthened.

Emotional arousal

A high state of emotional arousal can sometimes imprint experiences in long-term memory in a very detailed way. This is known as flashbulb memory.

The effects of brain damage

The most severe and permanent forms of memory impairment tend to be a result of brain damage. This can be due to disease, age, or physical trauma. The latter may be accidental, or the result of surgery.

Age

Memory quality declines gradually with age, but the pattern is far from simple.

Case study: brain infection

Viral brain infection can result in permanent memory damage, sometimes at very severe level. A famous case is that of Clive Wearing. Before his illness, he was a highly talented and successful musician. His brain was infected by the herpes simplex virus, a very common condition which normally does very little harm. In Mr Wearing's case, however, the virus attacked his hippocampus. This permanently prevented his short-term memory from transferring information to long-term memory.

Consequently, while he can remember things from before his illness, everything that has happened to him since then has only been stored in his short-term memory. This, of course, only has a duration of 15–30 seconds, and so Mr Wearing lives in a perpetual nightmare. This is known as anterograde amnesia. Where a patient can remember nothing from before brain damage occurred it is known as retrograde amnesia. Where you have one you usually have the other, but this was not so in Clive Wearing's case.[34,35]

Taking a behaviourist approach

The basis of the behaviourist perspective is that all behaviour, including mental behaviour, can be explained in terms of reward and punishment. If a particular behavioural form is rewarded it is likely to be repeated.

This approach can be applied to procedural memory. It is well established that skill performance is strengthened by conditioning. When an individual is learning a skill, they are first likely to learn it cognitively, by learning the set of rules. This will be stored in their declarative memory. At first the individual will have to think about every move they make. Gradually the process will become more and more automatic, as they receive the rewarding feeling of satisfaction at each stage of the process. Eventually the behaviour will be so conditioned that it will happen automatically. The movements must then be stored in a different memory store from the declarative memory store; that store is the **procedural memory.**

Taking a psychoanalytical approach

If failure to retrieve is not the result of brain damage, or of other sources mentioned in this book, then it may be the result of a deliberate act by our mind, to protect us from anxiety. This is known as **motivated forgetting.**

Repression
The balance between competing forces in our ego is a fragile one. A highly painful memory can threaten to cause the ego to lose control. According to Freud burying the memory out of reach in the unconscious is the subconscious mind's way of protecting the ego's balance.[36]

Tutorial

Practice questions
1. Name the four components of Baddeley and Hitch's model of short-term memory.

2. What are their functions?

3. Name as many types of memory as you can.

4. What is reconstructive memory?

5. What is confabulation?

6. What are the main sources of forgetting?

Seminar discussion
Can memory be improved? If so, how and by how much?

Course work, revision and exam tips
Don't fall for the fallacy that slow reading is careful reading. You've got to read at a speed by which the last parts of complex ideas enter your head before the first parts start to decay. That doesn't give you long – just 15 or 30 seconds. It is better to read quickly and read again than read slowly just once.

Read actively. Don't just read to soak up what the author has to say. Set out with questions to which you hope, or expect, the author will provide answers.

To speed up your reading, look for signpost devices such as 'The point is...', 'What I am saying is...', 'In short...' etc. These highlight the most important points the author is making.

Bibliographical notes

[1] Atkinson and Shiffrin 1971
[2] Craik and Lockhart 1972
[4] Shank and Ableson 1977
[5] See also Rumelhart and Norman 1985
[6] See also Cohen 1993
[8] See also Bartlett 1932
[9] See also Baddeley 1990
[10] Tulvin 1972
[11] See also Minsky 1975
[12] Baddeley and Hitch 1974
[13] Brown and Kulick 1977
[14] Tulvin 1985
[15] Pavio 1986
[16] Cohen and Squire 1980
[17] Neisser 1976
[18] Eysenck 1984
[19] Bransford et al. 1979
[20] Loftus and Zanni 1975
[21] Collins and Loftus 1975
[22] Baddeley 1975
[23] Salame and Baddeley 1982
[24] Baddeley 1995
[25] Baddeley 1996
[26] Cohen et al. 1986
[27] Tulvin 1972
[28] Loftus and Palmer 1974
[29] Hudspeth et al. 1964
[30] Underwood 1957
[31] Cohen 1986
[32] Blis and Lomo 1973 (cited in Kandel Schwartz and Jessell 1991)
[33] Hebb 1949
[34] Blakemore 1988
[35] Baddeley 1990
[36] Freud 1976

5

Intelligence

One minute summary – Intelligence can be defined in various ways. There are unitary and modular theories and qualitative and quantitative theories. There appears to be a centroid factor known as 'g'. There are various explanations of intelligence at the neural processing level. Debate continues as to how much intelligence is due to nature and how much to nurture. IQ is a measure of intelligence. Educated intelligence (crystallised intelligence) can be distinguished from natural intelligence (fluid intelligence).

In this chapter we will deal with:

▶ how intelligence is defined
▶ unitary theories of intelligence
▶ modular views of intelligence
▶ qualitative approaches towards intelligence
▶ enlarged models of intelligence
▶ the nature/nurture controversy
▶ IQ.

Learning objectives

After finishing this chapter you should know what each of the main schools of thought have contributed to our understanding of intelligence. You should then be able to tackle questions on intelligence from the following perspectives:

▶ behaviourist
▶ psychoanalytical
▶ cognitive
▶ psychobiological
▶ humanist

▶ social psychological.

You should know all the main theories and models of intelligence.

Defining intelligence

The concept of intelligence is defined in a variety of ways. Here are some examples:

▶ 'An individual is intelligent in proportion as he is able to carry on abstract thinking.' (Terman 1921).

▶ 'Innate, general cognitive ability.' (Burt 1955).

▶ '... aggregate of the global capacity to act purposefully, think rationally, to deal effectively with the environment.' (Wechsler 1944).

▶ 'The effective all-round, cognitive abilities to comprehend, to grasp relations and reason.' (Vernon 1969).

▶ '... an adaption ... it's function is to structure the universe.' (Piaget 1966).

▶ 'I view intelligence in context as consisting of purposive adaption to, shaping of, and selection of real world environments relevant to one's life.' (Sternberg 1984).

▶ 'Intelligence is what intelligence tests measure.' (Miles 1957).

The definitions fall into unitary or modular categories. The unitary definitions conceptualise intelligence as something we can measure on a uni-dimensional scale, such as an IQ test. Modular definitions view intelligence as comprising a range of separate abilities.

Unitary theories

There have been a number of theories based on an assumption that there is a single, **centroid** factor in intelligence.

The g factor

There is substantial evidence that intelligence has a principal component, plus a range of special factors. The principal component is often referred to as g, short for **neogenesis**. The special factors are often referred to as s factors.[1]

Models

Burt and Vernon found major and minor group factors lying between the g and s factors.

▶ The major group factors denote what some, but not all, tests measure.

▶ The minor group factors are what specific tests measure regardless of situation. The specific factors are those factors which are measured by specific tests in particular situations.[2]

What is g?

Spearman's assumption seems to be that g is a trait for making mental relationships between things.

Modular views on intelligence

Modular views are centred around the assumption that there is not just one intelligence faculty, but many. This kind of approach can explain 'dissynchronous' intellectual gifts, in other words the existence of giftedness in some areas, but not in others.

Thurstone

Thurstone found evidence of seven primary mental abilities, in addition to the g factor.[3,4] They are:

1. spatial
2. perceptual
3. numerical reasoning
4. verbal reasoning
5. word fluency
6. memory
7. inductive reasoning.

Guilford

Guilford devised a sophisticated, modular model of the structure of the intellect. It involved combinations from ranges of four kinds of content, five kinds of operations and six kinds of required results, to make a model of 120 separate mental abilities.[5] They are:

▶ content – figural, symbolic, semantic and behavioural

▶ operations – cognition, memory, divergent thinking, convergent thinking and evaluation

▶ products – units, classes, relations, systems, transformations and implications.

Cattell

Cattell distinguished between fluid intelligence and crystallised intelligence. Fluid intelligence is the innate ability to educe relations. He argued that it matures as the nervous system matures up to adulthood and, thereafter, it steadily deteriorates. Crystallised intelligence is based on learning, and so increases throughout life.[6]

Qualitative approaches

Piaget's developmental approach is concerned with intelligence as a process, rather than a quantity. More will be said about this later (page 51).

Enlarged models

Sternberg's triarchic theory of intelligence seeks to explain intelligence at a contextual and process level, as well as in terms of interaction between the two. In this theory, intelligence represents the effectiveness with which an individual deals with novel situations, and the degree to which they tend to automatise routine information processing.

Sternberg's model comprises a combination of: '... knowledge acquisition, performance and meta-components.'[7]

The nature/nurture controversy

The role of nature
It is generally accepted that intelligence levels depend on the influence of both genetics and environment. Genetics are believed to play the greater part. There is much evidence that the role of genetics is about twice as important as environmental influence.

The role of nurture
To Piaget, the development of intelligence is a process of adaption to the environment. Environmental factors are thus naturally influential in it. Intelligence exists in the form of schemata formation, the internalised impressions of the external world.

According to Piaget, an infant has no knowledge at birth. It develops its mental structures of knowledge by internalising what the senses tell it.[8] This would suggest a 100% environmental influence, so far as knowledge is concerned, but knowledge is only the crystallised part of intelligence.

Piaget distinguished three main influences in the development of intelligence:

1. maturation of the nervous system
2. our interaction with physical environment
3. influence of the social milieu.[8]

Heritability
The heritability issue in respect of intelligence is not quite as simple as saying that intelligent parents have intelligent children. There are things which complicate the picture, but not enough to render it unpredictable.

Intelligence is carried on dominant genes while dullness is carried on recessive genes. Consequently, the offspring of unions between close relatives tend to have significantly lower IQs than their parents. Eysenck refers to this phenomenon as the **inbreeding depression**.[9]

Eysenck also cites the **hybrid vigour** in which the reverse is the case. This features in the offspring of unions of mixed race. It occurs because related people have similar recessive genes, while racially different ones do not.

What is IQ?

The term IQ stands for **intelligence quotient**. It used to be measured by the formula:

$$IQ = \frac{\text{mental age}}{\text{chronological age}} \times 100$$

However, it now tends to be measured by reference to a mean and scaled in terms of standard deviations. This is known as **deviation IQ**.

Predictive power

There is much evidence that IQ tests are successful predictors of educational attainment. That is, after all, what crystallised intelligence is – educated intelligence.

IQ – Reading	0.61
IQ – Mathematics	0.72

Figure 2. Correlations between IQ and school attainment.

▶ *Key point* – IQ measures are not absolute units of intelligence. IQ is not an ordinal scale. IQ scores are, rather, comparisons with the mean.

Critics of IQ testing

IQ testing has many critics. Accusations of bias – cultural, ethnic, gender, and social class – are frequently levelled. Even the major **psychometric** authorities admit that a small degree of bias affects all tests.

However, stringent efforts are continuously being made to counter this problem. As at the present time the problem is acceptably small.

Tutorial

Practice questions

1. List Thurston's seven primary mental abilities.

2. List Guilford's four kinds of content, five kinds of operations and six kinds of results.

3. What is the difference between fluid intelligence and crystallised intelligence?

4. How does Sternberg's triarchic model of intelligence differ from all the others?

Seminar discussion

1. Is intelligence a useful concept?

2. How useful are IQ tests, and to whom?

Course work, revision and exam tips

When making notes, write on one side only of your notepad pages. You might want to compare ideas side by side at some point.

How much should you write? The most you should need to write is half a page of notes per one hour lecture, or per chapter of a book.

Bibliographical notes

[1] Spearman 1967
[2] Vernon 1971
[3] Thurstone 1938
[4] Thurstone 1947
[5] Guilford 1967
[6] Horn and Cattell 1967
[7] Sternberg 1984
[8] Richmond 1970
[9] Eysenck 1979

Emotions

One minute summary – Emotions can be analysed in various ways: primary types, component parts, negative/positive, and intensity. The behaviourist says we learn mixes of three basic emotions and store them with the situations from which they arise. Psychoanalysts believe emotions derive from threats to the ego. Cognitive psychologists generally accept that social and other clues determine our emotional experiences, and the level of arousal its intensity. Other causal theories include feedback from facial expressions and perceived cause of the situation. Some emotions involve the same physiological arousal. Experiencing emotion involves our nervous system, endocrine system and various hormones. Emotion can also be seen as a socially constructed safety valve. Humanists believe that anxiety occurs when an individual's personal integrity is threatened.

In this chapter we will deal with what emotions are, and how each school of thought treats them:

- ▶ the behaviourist
- ▶ the cognitive psychologist
- ▶ the humanist
- ▶ the psychoanalyst
- ▶ the psychobiologist
- ▶ the social psychologist.

Learning objectives

When you have finished this chapter, you should know what each of the main schools of thought has contributed to our understanding of emotions. You should then be able to tackle questions on emotions from various psychological viewpoints.

You will also know something of all the main theories and models of emotions.

What are emotions?

While the mind alone can provide us with an understanding of things, emotions give us a physical feeling about them so that we may wish to repeat the experiences, or avoid them. Without emotions we would be rather like robots.

▶ *Key definition* - emotions are responses to events.

Emotions have three aspects:

1. the experience
2. the physiological changes
3. the behaviour.

Classifying emotions

As in all science, one of the first things we have to try to do is describe and classify that which we are investigating. Emotions have been classified in various ways:

▶ pleasantness – unpleasantness[1]
▶ relaxation – tension[2]
▶ calm – excitement[3]
▶ acceptance – rejection[4]
▶ activation – control.[5]

Primary emotions

Plutick has identified eight primary emotions:[6]

1. surprise
2. fear
3. disgust
4. anger

5. joy
6. sorrow
7. acceptance
8. expectancy.

Stress emotions

The following tend to be classed as the stress emotions: [7]

▶ anger
▶ anxiety
▶ depression
▶ grief.

▶ guilt
▶ jealousy
▶ shame

Positive emotions

Positive emotions can be seen as having four dimensions:[8]

1. absorption
2. potency
3. altruism
4. spiritual.

Intensity of emotion

Emotions can be felt with different levels of intensity. It has been suggested that fear, for example, moves through the following stages:[9]

1. prudence
2. self restraint
3. caution
4. apprehension
5. anxiety
6. anguish
7. panic
8. terror.

You will see that anxiety is shown as a category of fear. This is because fear is a basic emotion from which other, more subtle emotions derive.

▶ *Study tip* – the essence of this book is to make sense of the different ways in which psychological issues are treated.

Let's consider these different viewpoints one by one.

Taking a behaviourist approach

▶ *Key point* – behaviourists focus only on observable behaviours. They assume they are learned by reward and punishment.

The emotions we start with
J.B.Watson, the founder of this school of thought, proposed that infants begin life with three basic emotions:

FEAR	RAGE	LOVE

Increasing the emotional range
As they develop, they learn that different things bring on different levels and mixtures of these feelings. Their range of emotional experiences thus becomes greater and more sophisticated.

Our brains store everything that happens to us together with the emotions we feel as a result.[10] Consequently, when we expect a similar event to take place we expect similar feelings to result.

When things go wrong
Sometimes things go wrong.

▶ *Example* – When a frightening event is taking place, a non-frightening object can become wrongly stored along with the memory of that fear. This can happen when the unrelated object is picked up by our peripheral vision, but escapes the notice of our conscious mind. Any subsequent appearance of the innocent object, which just happened to be in the line of our peripheral vision, will cause us to relive the fear.

Taking a psychoanalytical approach

▶ *Key point* – the psychoanalyst looks behind observable behaviour.

They begin with the assumption that all psychological conditions and behaviours are rooted in the defence of the ego, protecting it from guilt and anxiety.

Anxiety
According to Freud, anxiety is an instinctive kind of fear of separation from, or loss of, something crucial to the individual's

psychological well-being. The first separation an individual experiences is the separation from its mother's body, at birth.

Otto Rank argued that the traumatic feelings produced by this first separation are stored in the brain along with the memory. Thereafter, any threat of separation from, or loss of, a loved person or object will result in the individual reliving that anxiety to some degree.

Situations which produce anxiety
Various kinds of separations loom threateningly throughout our lives. A child learns the looks which go with rejections. It comes to feel anxious when it receives them. Marriage break-ups are one of the major separations which many people experience in life. Other examples are the death of a loved one, graduation, and retirement (separation from the workplace).

Differences between the psychoanalytical schools of thought
Rank's view was that the birth trauma is the most important source of anxiety.

Freudian psychoanalysts held a different view. To them the most fundamental fear of loss which shapes the lives of males after the birth trauma is irrational fear of castration by the father. This is known as the Oedipus Complex. After the child's mind has dealt with this conflict he ceases to be consciously aware it ever existed.

Adler's school of psychoanalysis held insecurity to be the central source of anxiety.

Positive emotions
Freud held that love is simply sublimated sex drive. At maturity, he believed a person's attachment to their opposite sex parent is converted to an attachment to a husband, or wife.

Increasing the emotional range
Psychoanalysts believe that by the time a child is five, it has probably experienced every kind of emotion there is at its most intense level.[11]

The competition with its same sex parent for its opposite sex parent's love will have produced anxiety. At times of closeness with the mother the child will have experienced joy, and at times of separation, sadness. When it has been told off it will have felt rejection. When it has been forgiven it will have felt acceptance. It will have also felt anger when it has been frustrated in its wishes. These are only a few examples.

All such feelings become stored, together with the events which give rise to them. They are relived whenever something jolts them into consciousness, for example the experience of a similar event. Sometimes we can relive, or feel, the emotional aspects without remembering the situations which brought them about.

Unique personal norms

Kubie argued that a kind of 'default position' is set up in the early years of life. This becomes the emotional state to which the individual tends to naturally return. If, because of traumatic childhood conditions, this is an unpleasant state, the individual will spend much of their time and energy trying to avoid it. They will not only do this consciously, but will also use preconscious and unconscious techniques, like denying or distorting truths which make them feel uneasy.

Psychoanalysts explain phobia differently from behaviourists. They hold that the anxiety arising from an intolerable situation is transferred to a situation which is more tolerable. Consequently, people feel extreme distress in situations that do not warrant such level of fear.

Taking a cognitive approach

▶ *Key point* – the cognitive psychologist focuses on the mental processes that take place when a person responds to something.

Two factor theory of emotion

It is now widely accepted that emotions have two causal factors:

1. physiological arousal

2. cognitive interpretation.

Schacter injected people with adrenaline to arouse them physiolo-

gically, and gave them different information about the effect it
would have on them. Also, some were placed in the company of
someone 'acting' happy, and others with someone 'acting' sad. He
found that the type of emotions they felt appeared to be determined
by the information and clues they were given. Most notably it was
by the clues from the happy or sad 'actor'. The level of arousal
determined the intensity of the emotion.[12]

Schacter's study did have some weaknesses, and it has not been
replicated. However, other studies have lent support to this view of
things.[13]

Earlier theories

Prior to Schacter's theory, it had been believed that the cognition
and physiological arousal components of emotions were independent of each other. Both were thought to be necessary though for an
emotion to be felt. Before then, it was believed that emotions were
simply responses to physiological behaviour. It was thought, for
example, that we become frightened *because* we run, not the other
way round. Several experimenters showed this theory was
incorrect.[14]

Recent theories
Facial feedback
Recent experiments have suggested that the determining factor in
emotions is actually facial expression.[15]

Weiner's attributional theory
This is a very recent development in cognitive theories. It holds that
emotion is determined by attribution. The first effect is perception of
whether an event is good or bad. Then evaluation of the cause
shapes the emotion. If the event is bad, for example, and thought to
be due to external causes, the emotion felt is anger.

Taking a psychobiological approach

▶ *Key point* – the psychobiologist focuses on the physiological and
chemical processes which take place inside us when we
respond to something.

Emotions which share a common factor

Although some emotions have physiological factors peculiar to them, many share a common physiological component with others. Love and hate are examples. How often have you watched a romantic film where the main character's attestations of hatred against their ex-lover suddenly give way to a passionate embrace?

Love and hate share the same physiological arousal, but not the same mental interpretation. This is also the case with happiness and anger. An example of two fundamental emotions which don't share a physiological component is anger and fear.[16]

Let's dig a bit deeper into this.

The chemicals

What is the chemistry underlying these physiological arousal states? The main factors are two *hormones* known as catecholamines:

adrenaline   noradrenaline

In fear the principal chemical released is adrenaline. In pain it is noradrenaline. Mixtures of these two provide the signals for various types of emotion.[17]

These hormones come from the adrenal glands situated just above the kidneys. They produce these substances when a 'messenger chemical' known as adrenocorticotrophic hormone (ACTH) reaches them. It comes from a small structure in the brain called the pituitary gland.

The nerve structure of emotions

The automatic nervous system (ANS) makes its effect on the internal organs such as the heart, lungs, and stomach by acting on their muscle coats, or by stimulating secretions from glands.

The system has two main parts – the sympathetic nervous system (SNS), and the parasympathetic nervous system (PNS). The sympathetic nervous system is involved in active emotions, like anger. The parasympathetic nervous system is involved in passive emotions, like sadness. The ANS causes the adrenal glands to produce adrenaline and noradrenaline. This, in turn, stimulates the ANS elsewhere in the body.

The brain

Gainotti[18] found that the right hemisphere of the brain seems to be the more sensitive to negative emotions. Psychosomatic pains – those which are 'all in the mind' – usually tend to occur on the left side of the body. It is this side that is controlled by the right hemisphere. The right of the brain also seems to be involved in perception of the emotional feelings of other people.

Stress

Things can go wrong. Normally, the whole system is under the control of the cerebral cortex, but it can lose control in situations of extreme emotion. If this happens the hypothalamus is left in control of the system and this does not operate in a rational way. In such circumstances it simply picks up the messages of arousal from the internal organs and stimulates them further in response.

Any type of emotion can become subject to this effect. Consider, for example, blind love, rage and crimes of passion.

If stress continues

If the source of stress continues, catecholamine production decreases, but stress hormone production increases. These have the purpose of resisting the effects of stress, but eventually the body's resources become depleted and physical illness results.

The stress hormones have not been explored in this text because their functions are essentially physiological rather than psychological.

Taking a social psychological approach

▶ *Key point* – Social psychologists focus upon social causes and consequences of individual human actions.

Averill's social theory

Averill argued that emotions are physiological effects interpreted in a social context. To be more specific, he sees them as transitory social roles determined by a person's undestanding of the situation. This kind of role permits the breakdown of social norms. They could, therefore, be seen as serving a safety valve function in the restrictive nature of social life.

Societies differ in the extent to which they allow this safety valve to function, that is, the degree to which they will accept that individuals are not always wholly responsible for all their actions.

Taking a humanist approach

▶ *Key point* – the humanist assumes it is necessary to look at the whole person, not just some aspect of them. This approach also credits individuals with free will and the capacity for voluntary change.

Self actualisation
Maslow argued that the desire for self actualisation is the ultimate aim of people. When self actualisation is threatened they become anxious.

Fear of rejection
Maslow believed people conceal their feelings because they fear rejection if they express them. This would, of course, threaten their self actualisation. Fear of rejection comes from past memories of times when emotional expression was met with rejection.

Tutorial

Practice questions
1. State at least two ways in which emotions can be analysed.

2. What are the two factors in Schacter's two-factor theory of emotions?

3. List four dimensions of positive emotions.

4. Give an explanation of emotion from a humanist perspective.

5. List the stress emotions.

6.   Why is stress dangerous to health?

Seminar discussion
Should we seek to control our emotions and, if so, to what degree?

Coursework, revision and exam tips
If an essay question seems straightforward you should consider that you might well have misinterpreted it.

Underline the key terms. Split the question into parts and bracket them. Ask not only *what is the question asking for?* but also *what is it not asking for?* This will help you focus and avoid missing the point.

Bibliographical notes

[1]   Osgood 1966, Schlosberg 1941
[2]   Schlosberg 1941(although the former referred to sleep rather than relaxation)
[3]   Wundt 1896
[4]   Schlosberg 1941
[5]   Osgood 1966
[6]   Ekman *et al.* 1972, Ekman and Freisen 1975, Plutchik 1980
[7]   Lazarus 1976
[8]   Argyle and Crossland 1987
[9]   Mira, E. cited in Casson 1965
[10]   Harris 1970
[11]   Harris 1970
[12]   Schacter 1964, Schacter and Singer 1962, Schacter and Wheeler 1962
[13]   Dutton and Aron 1974, Speisman *et al.* 1964
[14]   Cannon 1927, Sherrington 1900
[15]   Ekman *et al.* 1983
[16]   Ax 1953
[17]   Schacter and Singer 1962

7

Motivation

One minute summary – The psychobiological perspective on motivation focuses on drive theories. The cognitive approach identifies such things as competence, curiosity, cognitive consistency and achievement motives. The social psychological approach includes dramaturgical factors and the analysis of helping behaviour. The humanistic psychology of motivation focuses on such models as Maslow's 'hierarchy of needs'. The 'optimum level of arousal' theory proposes that we seek the optimum level of arousal – not too low and not too high.

In this chapter we will discuss what motivation is, and how each school of thought views it:

▶ behaviourist
▶ cognitive
▶ humanist

▶ psychoanalytical
▶ psychobiological
▶ social psychology

Learning objectives

By the time you have finished this chapter you should know what contributions to understanding of motivation are made by each of the main schools of thought. You should then be able to:

1. successfully tackle questions on motivation from various psychological viewpoints

2. understand all the main theories and models of motivation

What is motivation?

The word motivation comes from the Latin word *movere*, meaning to move. Motivation is therefore about the application of motive forces and how they translate into human behaviour.

Many different human motives have been identified.[1] They can be categorised into:

internal and external	innate and learned
cognitive and mechanistic	conscious and unconscious

All theories of human motivation are based on the pleasure principle.

▶ *Key definition* – the pleasure principle is that human beings and animals seek to gain pleasure, and avoid pain.

Taking a behaviourist approach

▶ *Key point* – Behaviourists explain motivation in terms of reward and punishment, in other words the satisfaction of drives, or deprivation of needs.

Drive reduction theory
Motives can be split into **psychogenic drives** and **physiological needs**. Psychogenic motives appear to be learned, while physiological motives appear to be innate. According to Hull, drives result from an internal disequilibrium. The body's demand for food, for example, is not matched by supply when the mind experiences the feeling of hunger. Learning by conditioning, he argues, is not possible without a drive reduction.[2]

Weakness of drive reduction theory
Drive reduction theory does not explain all motivation. Hunger, for example, is not a sufficient condition for eating. The classic example is the anorexic, but there are others less extreme. Nor is it a necessary condition. For example, many people eat through habit, for anxiety avoidance, or because of taste.

Negative drives

Besides being motivated by the pursuit of pleasure, individuals are also motivated to avoid pain and anxiety. The latter kind of motivation is known as **negative reinforcement.**

Coercion is a form of this negative reinforcement. The individual fears punishment if they do not perform particular actions. Phobias are another type of negative reinforcement. Here, the behaviour is intended to avoid anxiety caused by the phobia object. These are known as secondary drives. This is because the phobia itself only causes anxiety because it has become associated with another object, or situation of fear.

Taking a psychoanalytical approach

In psychoanalytical theory, avoidance of anxiety is a prime motivator of human behaviour. All experiences of separation from our parents, as children beginning with the great physical separation of birth itself, create anxiety. We thus seek to avoid separation, for example, isolation, or rejection, throughout our lives, to avoid reliving those early feelings.[3]

So we refrain from behaviour of the type which resulted in acts of rejection and isolation in childhood. This provides us with a stock of motivational resources for a successful and adaptive life.

Taking a cognitive approach

Sources of motivation which interest cognitive psychologists are:

▶ competence motives
▶ curiosity motives
▶ cognitive consistency needs

Competence motives

The competence motive is the will to have freedom of action, to be in control of one's life and destiny[3,4]. A fundamental difference between this kind of motive and most others is that it is not subject to drive reduction. The more competent and free a person becomes, the more competent and free they want to be.

The curiosity motive

Human beings are motivated by curiosity.[7] We respond to this drive by exploratory activity. In childhood, play provides an outlet for this drive.[5]

Cognitive consistency drive

Human beings have a drive to reduce what is known as **cognitive dissonance**. This is a discrepancy between thought and behaviour.[8]

▶ *Example* – A typical example of how this manifests itself is as follows. In the correctional policies sometimes used by ruling regimes in countries which have undergone a political revolution former dissidents are made to do work consistent with the ruling party's ideals. This is a theoretically sound strategy, for if their behaviour becomes consistent with ideological party loyalty, then their attitude must follow suit in order to prevent cognitive dissonance.

In addition to the need for consistency between thought and behaviour, there is a need for consistency between thought and thought. We tend to be different people in different social settings. We may fulfil one role in one setting, but another elsewhere. We play a number of parts, and some discrepancy is inevitable. The drive to reduce the discrepancy between our component selves is an important source of motivation.

Taking a social psychological approach

To a large degree, people behave in accordance with what people expect of them. Living among other people means playing a part in an ongoing social drama. All dramas involve roles for actors, and the social drama is no different. Each role comes with a traditional script, dictating the way the actor will behave and even their expected attitudes.

The details of our expected roles are called **norms.** If people do not stick fairly closely to the scripts for the roles they are playing they will not be taken seriously by others.[9]

▶ *Example* – A chartered accountant would have little or no credibility if he regularly turned up for work with visible tattoos, a ring in his nose and wearing jeans and beads. A youth worker, on the other hand, would probably not be taken seriously if he wore a business suit.

All members of a society learn which norms of behaviour are associated with particular roles – at least the more common ones. By the time we reach adulthood, we have watched the *real* social drama many times, and become highly skilled critics.

People can, and naturally do, criticise people who perform their roles implausibly. They notice the slightest things which are inconsistent. If sufficient, they will cause them to doubt the credibility of the person concerned, in the particular role they are performing. They may not always know exactly that it is that makes them doubt it, though. There is pressure, therefore, on people to make modest claims about themselves and to be modest in the roles they assume.[9]

'Helping' behaviour

When another human being is seen to be suffering, individuals may feel an urge to help. They do not always do so, though. What motivational force determines whether one individual will help another? It seems there are two key factors:[10,11]

1. the level of arousal
2. costs and/or reward.

The more deserving the case, the more emotional arousal an onlooker will experience.

▶ *Example* – A raggedly dressed adult, smelling of alchohol and lying ill at the side of the road, would be unlikely to attract the same level of emotional response in onlookers as would be the case if it was a child. Similarly, a lame beggar is likely to attract more support than an able-bodied one.

Anticipated costs or rewards for helping may be very tangible. For example, helping the enemy in times of war will lead to ostracism, or worse. Finding and returning something lost by a wealthy person could result in a financial reward. However, the costs and/or rewards are normally much more subtle. Helping a drunk who has fallen over may result in being attacked or being vomited over (cost). Helping an old person who has collapsed is likely to win the approval of others and gratify one's conscience (reward).

Pluralistic ignorance
Apparent apathy among people, when someone in their midst appears to need help, may be partly due to the fact that onlookers are unsure of whether they should step in to help. Seeing others not interfering – perhaps for the same reason – may suggest to them that help is not required, or not appropriate.[12]

Diffusion of responsibility
Another force which may inhibit helping action may come from the fact that onlookers consider there are plenty of others present to help and so they are, themselves, relieved of responsibility.[13]

Taking a humanist approach

The humanist sub-discipline has made helpful contributions to this area of knowledge, particularly where motivation in work situations is concerned. The most prominent contributor has been Maslow.

Maslow's hierarchy of needs
Maslow proposed that human needs could be hierarchically ordered in terms of seven levels. It is, in fact, more a pyramid of needs.[14] The levels are as shown in Figure 3.

In Maslow's model, individuals must satisfy one level before proceeding to the next. If a person's safety needs, for example their need for a reliable source of income, are not met, that individual will not be motivated by the provision of status symbols like a job title or a company car.

Satisfaction of each level of needs becomes more difficult the higher they are in the pyramid. Rewards attached to fulfilment becomes progressively more **intrinsic** and less **extrinsic**. At the most

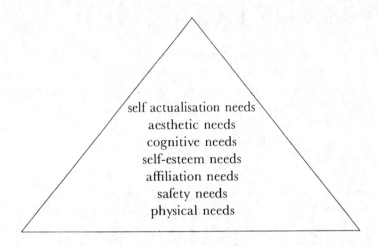

self actualisation needs
aesthetic needs
cognitive needs
self-esteem needs
affiliation needs
safety needs
physical needs

Figure 3. Maslow's hierachy of needs. The most basic needs
are at the base of the pyramid.

basic level, our needs are biological. Before anything else a person
needs enough food and drink to survive and a place of shelter in
which to sleep. Providing this level is satisfied an individual is
motivated, next, to looking after their safety. At the third level lie
affiliation needs: being accepted as part of a social group, or groups,
has great psychological importance.

Achievement need

Research on achievement need has been mainly associated with
McClelland.[15] Achievement need is an unconscious drive. Individuals with a high level of achievement need tend to have the
following traits:

▶ they attribute performance to internal factors
▶ they are persistent
▶ they prefer to work with experts than friends.

The need for freedom of action

One of the things which spurs people to action is a threat to their
freedom of operation. People differ, to some degree, in their
tolerance of control by others.[16]

Taking a psychobiological approach

Psychobiologists' interest in motivation has tended to focus upon the basic drives, those at the bottom level of Maslow's hierarchy of needs - hunger and thirst, for example. They employ two main types of theory:

▶ homeostatic drive theories
▶ drive reduction theories.

The needs for food and drink are known as homeostatic drives, because their purpose is to maintain a constant supply of energy and fluid, a situation known as homeostasis.

The basic assumption underlying drive reduction theories is that when supply and demand in the body's physiological resources gets out of balance, the individual will take action to redress it. When there is insufficient energy, for example, to meet demands an individual will obtain food and eat.

Where are the control centres?

Eating seems to be largely controlled in our hypothalamus. Different centres, however, seem to control eating on the one hand and cessation of eating on the other. The trigger for eating appears to be in the lateral hypothalamus (usually referred to as LH).[17,19] Other parts of the brain appear to be involved, too. They are the:

▶ amygdala
▶ thalamus
▶ hippocampus
▶ frontal lobe.

The control for cessation, or slowing down of eating appears to be in the ventromedial hypothalamus (the lower central part of the hypothalamus usually referred to as the VMH).[18]

The pleasure centre of the brain appears to lie in the medial forebrain bundle. The agents for controlling it seem to be the neurotransmitters dopamine and noradrenaline. The conditions which bring about hunger appear to differ from those which cause satiety, or no longer feeling hungry. While energy level, and need for nourishment of a particular type make us hungry and want to eat, it cannot be changes in these which make us want to stop eating. The nourishment and energy does not reach its targets until sometime after we have ceased to feel hungry. Digestion is slow.

The leaky barrel model
What is known as the 'leaky barrel' model assumes that the body does not have a target level for energy intake, so that hunger ceases when it is reached. Instead, it suggests there is a settling point, around which weight tends to settle in spite of variation in food intake. It is called the leaky barrel model because it is assumed that weight beyond that set level will tend to be rapidly lost. The lateral hypothalamus appears to be involved in establishing weight targets, or levels.[19]

Stretch receptors
The hypothalamus appears to receive signals to control eating from a number of sources:

▶ stretch receptors in the stomach[27]
▶ gastric branch of the vegus nerve[28]
▶ CCK receptors in the duodenum[29]
▶ CCK receptors in the peripheral nervous system.[21]

Glucostatic theory
Glucoreceptors are devices which detect the level of glucose in our bloodstream. Glucose is extremely important to the functioning of the body. Some say that these are the most important triggers of eating behaviour. It has been established that they are situated in the ventromedial hypothalamus (VMH).[23]

Eating is controlled by insulin utilisation and this in turn is controlled by the hypothalamus.

Lipostatic theory
Lipostatic theory proposes that we all have a set level around which our weight tends to fluctuate.[22] This would account for why weight losses from dieting are generally not very permanent and often short lived.

Both glucostatic and lipostatic theories assume there is a set point, or level, for stored energy in the body, against which actual levels are compared by the processing system that controls motivation to eat. The glucostatic theory explains the short-term, and the lipostatic theory the long-term, effects.[22]

Sensory-specific satiety

In the lateral hypothalamus, neurons have been discovered which are sensitive to particular tastes. Furthermore, they are subject to the effects of habituation. Habituation is when repeated amounts of a stimulus reduce the level of sensitivity to it. This processing of motivation according to tastes could account for obesity.[25]

What motivates us to drink?

Before beginning to attempt an answer to this question it is important to note that there are two fundamentally different types of thirst:

▶ **Osmometric thirst** is a response to cellular dehydration. We need to drink when the fluid part of our cell cytoplasm is low.

▶ **Volumetric thirst** occurs when blood plasma and cerebro-spinal fluid has fallen to a low (hypertonic) level. This may occur as a result of blood loss. When this happens fluid is drawn out of the cells and this leaves a deficit there. This deficit is experienced as osmometric thirst. This makes us want to drink.

The mechanisms regulating motivation to drink include stomach distension and, perhaps, a mouth metering system. The latter may compare the deficit in fluids, and, therefore, the amount of liquid the body needs to take in, with the amount actually drunk. There are also measurement mechanisms known as osmoreceptors, in the lateral preoptic areas of the hypothalamus (LPH).

The 'dry mouth' theory of thirst

If a dry mouth were sufficient to explain motivation to drink it would not explain drinking to excess as humans and other animals sometimes do.

Satiety is taste specific. Our desire for a drink with a particular taste e.g. coffee may be satiated, while our desire for another e.g. tea is not. If fluid deficits were the main source of motivation it wouldn't matter what the flavour was.

The 'positive incentive' theory of drinking

The positive incentive theory of drinking suggests that dehydration increases the incentive value of drink.[22,25] Imagine how good plain water tastes in the searing heat of a holiday in a sunny climate. If a period of deprivation has increased the incentive value of a drink above that which it usually has, then an individual will drink more than they need. This is because the signal for cessation will not be sent until the incentive value decreases to a level where there is no further incentive to drink.

The 'optimum level of arousal' theory of motivation

The optimum level of arousal theory of motivation explains it in terms of individuals seeking an optimum level of arousal. If arousal is too low we seek situations which give us what is known as an *autonomic jag* – a stimulus to the autonomic nervous system. If arousal is too high there will be sensory overload and we will avoid the situation, to reduce arousal. Sensory deprivation has negative psychological effects. If severe, they can include hallucinations. An example of flight from sensory overload is where people who have received a severe emotional shock tend to deny the situation to themselves.[28,29,30,31]

Tutorial

Practical exercises

1. List at least four parts of the brain involved in eating behaviour.

2. What are glucostatic receptors?

3. What are lipostatic receptors?

4. What is sensory-specific satiety?

5. Name two kinds of thirst.

6. Which most closely describes the 'positive incentive theory of drinking'?

7. Tick which statement is correct:

☐ The more your body needs fluid the more you will drink.
☐ The more I drink, the more I get drunk.
☐ Dehydration increases the incentive value of drink.

Seminar discussion
To what extent do humans have free will?

Course work, revision and exam tips
When answering an essay question, define all key concepts. Interpret the question. Build your arguments logically. Elaborate them with appropriate examples. Present appropriate evidence. Attribute all knowledge you have used to the sources from which you acquired it. Include an accurate bibliography.

Bibliographical notes

[1] Murray 1938
[2] Hull 1943
[3] Rubin and McNeil 1983
[4] Brehm 1966
[5] Bem 1972
[6] Lepper and Greene 1978
[7] Butler 1954
[8] Festinger 1957
[9] Goffman 1971
[10] Piliavin et al. 1969
[11] Piliavin et al. 1981
[12] Latane and Rodin 1969
[13] Darley and Latane 1968
[14] Maslow 1954
[15] McClelland 1953
[16] Wortman and Brehm 1975
[17] Teitelbaum and Stellar 1954
[18] Teitelbaum 1967
[19] Anand and Brobeck 1951
[20] Olds and Milner 1954
[21] See Carlson 1992
[22] Pinel 1993
[23] Mayer 1955
[31] Mayer and Marshall 1956
[25] Rolls and Rolls 1982
[26] Rolls et al. 1980
[27] Wolkwilz et al. 1980
[28] Berlyne 1969
[29] Butler 1954
[30] Bexton et al. 1954
[31] Heron 1957

8

Child Development

One minute summary – Learning configures the brain in terms of schemata, which develop by assimilation, accommodation and equilibration. The three main cognitive development theorists are Piaget, Bruner and Vygotsky. Piaget identified four stages in development: sensory motor, pre-operations, concrete operations and formal operations. Bruner identified three modes of thinking in the developmental process: inactive, iconic and symbolic. Vygotsky identified an important point in development to be where speech and practical activity converge. He also identified what he called the 'zone of proximal development'. This is the difference between what a child can achieve, and what it can achieve with help. Freud identified anal, phallic, latency and genital stages of development. Erikson identified eight stages of development throughout life.

This chapter will deal with child development, as viewed from the following perspectives:

▶ cognitive
▶ psychoanalytical
▶ psycho-social.

Learning objectives

Once you have finished this chapter you will know:

1. what contributions to understanding child development are made by each of those schools of thought.

2. all the main theories and models of child development

This chapter deals with how children develop in terms of their thinking ability and their personality.

Taking a cognitive approach

The main contributors to our knowledge in respect of cognitive development are Piaget, Bruner and Vygotsky.

The main contributors in respect of the development of personality are Freud and Erickson.

Piaget

▶ *Key point* – to Piaget intelligence is a process of adaptation. Children develop knowledge through interacting with and adapting to their world.

Schemata theory
Schemata is the plural of schema. A schema is the internal, neural representation of knowledge of the external world. It is the configuration of activated circuitry in the brain as a result of experience. Schemata develop over time, increase in complexity and interconnect with other schemata.

Where does it all start? The answer is that the earliest motor responses – sucking, kicking, grasping, for example – are stored and gather complexity by variation of the behaviour. These stored, sensory, feedback data are the early forms of schemata.[1]

How schemata develop
Three processes are identified in schemata development: accommodation, assimilation, and equilibration.

▶ *Accommodation* – refers to changing the structures in our heads, i.e. the schemata, so the experiences we are perceiving will fit into them.

▶ *Assimilation* — refers to the way we distort our perceptions to bring about the final fit. At particular stages of our cognitive development, organisational processes take place where different schemata accommodate and assimilate other schemata. This is known as 'reciprocal assimilation'.

Learning is, thus, a process of both accommodation and assimilation. Each time we experience the same thing we approximate closer and closer to the actual external reality in the configuration of our schemata. The closer our schemata approximates to reality, the less internal adjustment and external distortion are necessary for identification and comprehension of an experience.

▶ *Equilibration* – This is the dynamic which causes accommodation and assimilation to take place. It is a drive to equalise the external with the internal world. When we experience something for the first time there is a high level of disequilibrium. This is because there is no internal structure which closely matches the experience we are having. The equilibration drive leads us to modify our internal structures and distort the experience until a match is achieved.

Some processes involve more accommodation than assimilation. In others, assimilation is paramount. For example, investigative work involves a relatively high degree of accommodation, while play involves a relatively high degree of assimilation. Practising psychomotor skills is more or less pure assimilation; it is the internal structures we have to change here, not the external ones. You would never learn to shoot straight if your mind tended to move the target.

At stages pretty rigidly set at age points in childhood, schemata integrate to form hierarchies.

Importance of errors
Piaget believed that the errors a child makes represent important windows on what is going on in their cognitive development.

The stages of development
According to Piaget's theory cognitive development takes place

according to a rigid sequence. There is no point in trying to help the child develop concepts at one level until those at the previous level have been mastered. The stages are as follows:

0-2 years	sensorimotor stage
2-7 years	pre-operations stage
7-11 years	concrete operations stage
11-15 years	formal operations stage.

Although the sequence is rigid, the age at which each new stage begins is not. Furthermore, some aspects of development straddle the boundary between two stages. Take for example the ability to understand instinctively that equal amounts taken from equal amounts leave equal remainders, regardless of how deceptive it looks graphically. This is known as 'conservation' or the ability to conserve. This ability manifests itself in different ways:

numbers	length
liquid quantity	weight
substance	volume
quantity	

Conservation in these different forms is mastered at different ages.

Type of conservation ability	*Approx. age of attainment*
Number and liquid	by around 7
Substance, quantity, length and weight	by ages 7 – 11
volume	by about 11

This staggering is known as **dècalage**. The pattern appears to hold true across all cultures.

The sensorimotor stage (0-2 years)
During this stage physical behaviour and thought are inseparable. Babies only think about what they are doing or sensing at the time.

▶ *Lack of object permanence* -- Furthermore, they are only aware of the existence of someone, or something when it is within the range of their senses (seeing, hearing, or touching). When such people, or things are out of sight to the child they don't exist.

▶ *Egocentricism* - Piaget argued that young infants are highly egocentric. The world, as they know it revolves around them. The fact that when a young child puts its hands over its eyes and says to its parent, 'You can't see me' was, to Piaget, evidence of this.

▶ *Centration* – this means the tendency to classify things on the basis of a single characteristic. If the child learns that something with wheels is a car then it is likely to call a bicycle, or a wheelbarrow a car also.

▶ *Syncretic thought* – Closely allied to centration is syncretic thought. This is a tendency to resort to pairing on the basis of common characteristics in a series, due to inability to find characteristics common to the whole group. Vygotsky referred to this, too. He called it complexive thinking.

▶ *Transducive reasoning* – Transducive reasoning is drawing inferences on the basis of a single characteristic. This can lead to a kind of personification tendency known as animistic thinking. A child who has bumped its head on the corner of the table may say 'Naughty table'. This is because, when other children have hit the infant its mother has said they are naughty. The infant generalises from this. All forces which physically hurt it are thought of as naughty. The early part of this first stage of a child's life contains two identifiable sub-stages. They are the pre-conceptual stage (2-4 months) and the intuitive stage (4-7 months).

▶ *Invisible displacements* – At 4-8 months a child will visually track objects. At 6-7 months it will know that a whole object is present when it only sees a part.[5] This ability is known as invisible displacements. If it was completely obscured, however, it would not infer its presence behind whatever was screening it.

▶ *Person and object permanence* – To the very young child, what it cannot see does not exist. It has to develop an awareness that things remain in existence even when they are out of sight. This is known as object permanence. The permanence of people, even when out of sight, is known as person permanence. Person permanence tends to develop first. It is probably from this development that the child begins to be aware of object permanence. Piaget believed that object permanence tends to be fully developed by the time a child is a year old, but others say as early as eight months.

▶ *Deferred imitation* – From 18-24 months children are building up internal images of the world sufficient to enable them to start thinking. They will then begin to imitate behaviour they have witnessed in the past. This is known as deferred imitation.

Pre-operations stage (2 – 7 years)
In this stage the child's ability for abstraction is emerging, but its behaviour is still mainly orientated towards concrete objects and situations.

▶ *Pre-conceptual stage* – Between 2 and 4 years of age a child has difficulty in sequencing and difficulty in arranging heights. The latter is referred to as **seriation.**

▶ *Intuitive stage* – Between 4 and 7 years of age the child's logic tends to be poor. Its thinking tends to be absolutist, and relative terms tend to confuse it. Children still lack the ability to understand the relationship between parts and wholes. The latter is often referred to as distinguishing between super-ordinate and subordinate classes.

▶ *Decentring* – At five years of age decentring begins to occur. This means that the child starts to be able to categorise in terms of more than one feature. The development of this ability continues even into the formal operations stage.

▶ *Egocentricism* – Piaget claimed to have demonstrated that children are still egocentric at six years old. In his Swiss Mountains experiment, children were invited to sit on a model of a mountain and a doll was placed at some other position. The child was then shown pictures of what the doll might be seeing from where it was sitting. Four year olds would get the wrong answer every time, always choosing the picture representing what they themselves saw. Six year olds got it right sometimes, seven year olds got it right consistently.

Concrete operation stage (7-11 years)
Operations are mental actions. During this stage of development they cannot be carried out purely in the child's mind, but only with actual objects. Operations involve compensation, identity, and reversal.

▶ *Conservation* – Conservation abilities develop during this period (see page 80). Conservation of volume, however, might not occur until the child has moved into the next developmental stage (formal operations).

▶ *Part/whole relationships* – During this stage the child masters the ability to understand part/whole relationships.

▶ *Egocentricity* – The child increasingly learns to see things from the viewpoint of others.

▶ *Transitivity of height* – By the end of this stage of development, about 11 years of age, children have mastered the ability to order in terms of height.

▶ *The transition to formal operation stage* – In the last year of this stage, and the first year of the next, children become more investigative in their nature. They become more interested in how things work. Also, the influence of parents declines, and the approval of other significant adults and peers becomes more important to them.

Formal operations stage (11 – 15 years)
Formal operations refer to operations on *form* rather than *matter*. The formal operations child can manipulate things in its head. It can consider and discuss hypothetical situations.

▶ *Question* – How many reach formal operations stage?

It has been argued that only about a third of the population of the industrialised world ever reach the formal operations stage of development and that in some cultures few, if any, do.

Piaget claims that everyone reaches the formal operations stage, though. It may not occur on time; it may be delayed to until 20 years of age, but it will happen. It will not necessarily apply to all areas of cognitive ability, though; it depends on the experience and opportunities the individual has during that period of their life.

Piaget thought language might be a necessary condition for formal operations, but certainly not a sufficient one.

Piaget and play
Play, or make-believe, is an aspect of the 'general symbolic function' of cognitive development. It involves make-believe and representation. Its purpose is that of adaptation. It enables children to practise their competencies and deal with emotional conflicts.

Collective symbolism and role taking
Through collective symbolism and role taking, children act out and adapt to situations in a safe, acceptable way. Collective symbolism is a collective subscription to a common make-believe situation.

Language skill is important in play and play, in turn, offers opportunity for enhancement of language skill. Children practise speaking in linguistic styles which others would use.

Kinds of play
Different kinds of play can be identified:

▶ symbolic or make-believe
▶ mastery
▶ play with rules.

Children's conceptualisation of rules changes during their development.

Piaget made a distinction between intellectual activity and play.

Intellectual activity	*Play*
problem led	desire led
accommodation	assimilation

Play can also be distinguished from imitation. Up to the start of the formal operations stage of development, most play is pure assimilation and imitation is pure accommodation.

Weaknesses of Piaget's theory
Piaget's work has been widely criticised. Some of the main criticisms are a failure to take account of the influence of personal factors in development, and individual differences, lack of statistical analysis, unstandardised testing and types of tests and language used.

Bruner
Like Piaget, Bruner identified a changing pattern of cognitive activity as children develop. He presented three modes:

1. enactive mode
2. iconic mode
3. symbolic mode.[8]

During the enactive mode stage children's schemata are of the motor kind. From one and a half years of age until seven years of age a child's dominant mode of thinking is iconic. Icons are composites of images which are accumulated over time. Iconic mode children can reproduce images in their minds, but do not have the ability to restructure them.

Symbolic mode
The transition to symbolic mode occurs between the ages of six and seven. This corresponds with Piaget's transition from pre-operations stage to concrete operations stage. The symbolic mode child develops the ability to restructure images in its mind.

Bruner and Piaget compared
The main difference between Bruner and Piaget is in the role they

attribute to language. Bruner saw language as crucial to the symbolic mode of thought. Piaget saw it as merely an aspect, or by-product of this development, a tool which the child could use.

Vygotsky

Vygotsky's theory is, to some degree, a reverse of Piaget's. Rather than saying that cognitive development originates from within, and is brought out by interaction with the social environment, he argued that it originates in the social environment and is internalised into the mind. The influence of the Marxist assumptions about knowledge — characteristic of the culture in which Vygotsky was based – are not hard to detect.

An important convergence
The most important stage of cognitive development is, according to Vygotsky's theory, the stage at which the development of practical activity and speech converge.

Zone of proximal development
Vygotsky was interested not only in actual development, but in potential, too. He conceptualised what he called a 'zone of proximal development'. This is the difference between what a child can achieve and what it can achieve, with help.[9]

Taking a psychoanalytical approach

▶ *Key point* – Psychoanalytical theories of child development are theories about the development of the **ego**.

The Freudian theory

The dominant psychoanalytical theory is the Freudian one. According to Freud the psyche has three main parts, the id, the ego, and the superego.

▶ The **id** is the pure, selfish, desire instinct, which all animals have.

▶ The **ego** is the intelligent part of the consciousness, the part that manages the conflicting forces of desire and restraint.

▶ The **superego**. We live in societies in order to serve our wants more fully. However, being a social animal involves give and take. We have to, therefore, develop a force of restraint within us. This is known, in Freudian theory, as the superego. This is the stored inferences we make from what our parents say to us and to others during that stage of development when we do not have adequate critical abilities to evaluate those inferences. That is not to say that the development of the superego stops when we move on from that stage, but, overwhelmingly, the content of the superego contains the data from that period.

We would not survive long if we only listened to our id. Other people would not put up with someone who was not to a reasonable degree restrained by conscience. Furthermore, there is much instrumental sense in the influence of the superego. Parents know that by exercising restraint, the level of eventual rewards can be greater. People without a significant superego are known as **psychopaths,** or **sociopaths.** The lack of influence from the superego causes their behaviour to be selfish to a level which their community will simply not accept, or allow to continue.

Conversely, however, if an individual only listened to the demands of its superego, its behaviour would be so constrained that it would satisfy none of the demands of its id. The ego, therefore, is the intelligent management force of the psyche which balances the demands of the id and the superego. It does this in a way designed to get the optimum rewards for the id at minimum cost.

Five stages of development

Freud identified five stages in the development of the psyche. They are the:

1. oral stage
2. anal stage
3. phallic stage
4. latency stage
5. genital stage (sometimes known as urogenital stage).

Oral stage

The oral stage of development lasts until about the first year of life. During this stage the main source of sensory data is through the lips. This stage, itself, is divided into two. The early part is the *incorporative stage*. During this stage the baby's behaviour is passive. The second phase of the oral stage is an aggressive phase. Here, the baby tends to bite.

Anal stage

Between the ages of one and three a child is aware, and focuses upon, its ability to produce urine and faeces from its body. It is also aware of its ability to retain them, for it is being taught to do so by its parents. This stage, too, can be divided into two. In the first phase the focus is on expulsion of products, while in the second stage the focus is on retention. Up to this time the child had every reason to believe that its parents' love was unconditional. Now it has to face the fact that it is not. Love and praise are given on the condition that it performs as they want it to.

Phallic stage

Between the ages of three and six, children become aware of their genitals as a source of pleasure. They become aware, too, of differences between the genitals of males and females and all kinds of sex-related emotions begin to develop.

▶ *Oedipus complex* – Male children become jealous of their father's relationship with their mother. The feeling reaches a crisis point where the male child fears he will be castrated by the father. This fear is reinforced by the child's inference of the reason its sisters, or other, female children are anatomically different. This leads male children to repress their sexual feelings, and this heralds the start of the latency period.

▶ *Electra complex* – Freud's theory provides that female children have a sex-related crisis around this time, too, but it is different from that of male children. Males eventually identify with their father through fear of physical harm if they do not. Females come to identify with their mother, through fear of loss of love, because of their attachment to their father.

Latency period
During the latency period sexual feelings are put on hold. This allows the child to concentrate on developing important life skills.

Genital period
In the genital period psychosexual development is complete, according to Freudian theory. Here the individual focuses on sexual interaction with others.

Repression
Throughout childhood, the id and the superego are always in conflict and sometimes the conflict is so great that it is repressed. Repression means burying a feeling in the unconscious so that you are not aware of it. The effects of repression, however, rise to the surface in the form of neurosis.

Developmental crises
Crises occur at each stage of development. They are like cross-roads – which way does the child go from here? How is it to respond? The task at these points in time is to resolve the conflicts permanently. If they are not resolved the child will become **fixated** in that developmental stage.

The way a child is treated by parents has a bearing on whether conflicts will be resolved.

▶ *Example 1* – If in the oral stage a child has been deprived of the breast it will not want to move on, for it remains unsatisfied. If, on the other hand, it is made too comfortable in that stage, it will want to stay there.

▶ *Example 2* – In the anal stage, if the child has not had sufficient opportunity to satisfy its desire to produce bodily products as and when it wished, it will remain unsatisfied and will not want to move on to the next stage. Similarly, in the second part of that stage, if it has not received sufficient praise during potty training, it will want more and not be inclined to choose to move on at the cross-roads. On the other hand, if the anal stage has brought too great a level of reward, the child will want to stay there.

It is also possible that a child will suddenly regress to an earlier stage if the conditions of its current stage become too painful. This might occur, for example, if the harsh realities and personal responsibility of adult life make impossible demands on a person in a difficult situation. Regressing to an earlier stage would relieve the individual of the assumption of personal responsibility.

The most important developmental crisis of all, for males, is the Oedipus Complex and for females, the Electra Complex, after which each naturally tend to identify with their same sex parent. This will be dealt with further in Chapter 13 on Moral Development.

Taking a psycho-social approach

Erikson's theory[10] differs from Freud's. In the latter, development continues only until adolescence. Erikson, however, saw psycho-social development going on throughout life. Secondly, while Freud argued that the ego and superego develop after birth, in Erikson's theory both exist at birth. Thirdly, the psychic conflicts in Freudian theory are between the id and the superego. In Erikson's theory the conflicts are within the ego itself.

Erikson's eight stages of psycho-social development

Freud's theory contains only five stages of development. Erikson's, however, contains eight, extending throughout life. Each stage ends in an identity crisis involving a choice between two options. The pattern of the stages is in our genes. Erikson referred to this as the epigenetic principle.

If parents wean children from one stage to the next too early, the child will feel traumatised by sense of powerlessness. It may regress to the previous stage and become fixated there. Fixations in a particular stage have implications for a person's personality. For example, people fixated in the oral stage may be verbally spiteful, attention seeking and bossy as adults, and have thumb sucking, nail biting or skin biting habits. People fixated in the anal stage are likely to be either obsessively messy or obsessively tidy as adults. Things can be even more complex than this, for individuals may also develop a strong, opposite response in order to unconsciously mask an undesirable aspect of their personality.

Identity crises

In Erikson's theory, three important identity crises occur early in life. The first occurs at a stage between one and a half and three years of age, the second at starting school and the third at puberty.

Tutorial

Practice questions

1. List four kinds of conservation ability.

2. How could the language used in tests have biased Piaget's findings on the ages at which various conservation abilities appear in children?

3. List Bruner's three stages of cognitive development.

4. What is Vygotsky's zone of proximal development?

5. How useful is this concept?

6. What is the important convergence that Vygotsky referred to?

Seminar discussion

How useful are Piaget's findings in understanding child development?

Coursework, revision and exam tips

Keep to the word limits in your essays. Naive students sometimes think they should be praised for writing more than the word limits. Often, however, the extra amounts to excess words rather than additional ideas. There is an old Chinese saying about a person who wrote a long letter because he didn't have time to write a short one. Being concise is a skill you have to learn.

Bibliographical notes

[1] Piaget and Inhelder 1969
[2] Cammil and Smith 1978
[3] Bower 1977
[4] Donaldson and Mcgarrigle 1974
[5] but see Ginsburg 1981
[6] Borke 1975
[7] See Piaget 1973
[8] Bruner 1966
[9] Vygotsky 1978
[10] Erikson 1968

9

Language Development

One minute summary – Language has deep and surface structures. There is a reasonably consistent pattern of language development in humans. The common ways in which parents respond to their infant's speech is known as the Language Acquisition Support System (LASS). The left hemisphere of the brain tends to be the dominant one for language processing. The nature/nurture controversy can be tested by trying to teach language to non-humans. The key elements of Chomsky's theory are universal grammar, linguistic universals and the language acquisition device. Children seem to develop grammar on their own.

In this chapter you will learn about:

▶ the nature of language
▶ the chronology of language development
▶ the behaviourist view of language development
▶ the psychobiological view of language development
▶ the cognitive view of language development.

Learning objectives

Once you have finished this chapter you should:

1. know what contributions to understanding language development are made by each of the main schools of thought

2. be able to tackle questions on language development from several different psychological viewpoints

3. know all the main theories and models of language development.

The nature of language

Psychologists are interested in how language is acquired and what its role is in thinking and learning. This branch of psychology is known as **psycholinguistics.**

Scholars have endeavoured to identify important features of language. Hockett listed the following thirteen design features:[1]

1. vocal auditory channel
2. broadcast transmission and directional reception
3. rapid fading
4. interchangeability
5. total feedback
6. specialisation
7. semanticity
8. arbitrariness
9. discreteness
10. displacement
11. productivity
12. traditional transmission
13. duality of patterning.

Aitchison[2] suggested the following ten features:

1. vocal-auditory channel
2. arbitrariness of code
3. semanticity
4. cultural transmission
5. spontaneous usage
6. turn taking
7. duality
8. displacement
9. structure dependence
10. creativity.

The elements of language
The elements of language fall into two categories:

▶ sounds
▶ grammar.

Even if words are written, the sounds are implied.

Phonology
Phonology is the science of speech sounds. It is concerned with phones and phonemes.

▶ *Phones* are identifiable sounds of the most basic nature produced by the human speech system. Examples are: *b, c, d, e, etc.* There are more than just the vowels and consonants. For example, a Londoner will produce the sound *r* very differently to the way a Scottish person would pronounce it. The two sounds are different phones.

▶ *Phonemes* are the classes of phones which have a common meaning. The *r* produced by the Londoner and that produced by the Scottish person are, thus, elements of the same phoneme. Another example is the difference between a Cockney expression of the vowel *a* and the same vowel expressed by a person with a received English accent.

Morphology
Morphology refers to the rules for building phonemes into morphemes. Morphemes are words, suffixes and prefixes. Morphemes that depend for their meaning upon the words to which they are attached, e.g. prefixes and suffixes, are known as bound morphemes. Those which are not are known as unbound morphemes.

Syntax
Syntax refers to the rules for structuring words into a meaningful language.

Grammar
Grammar is the essence of human language. It comprises phonology, morphology, syntax and semantics.

Speech

Speech and language are different things. Speech does not necessarily require meaning. Language, on the other hand, does require meaning.

Deep and surface structures

Chomsky[3] argued that linguistic forms have both surface structures and deep structures.

▶ *Surface structures* are what can be understood by a literal translation of the communication.

▶ *Deep structures* are the extra meanings which can be gleaned by reference to other non-verbal and non-linguistic means, such as gestures, looks, tone of voice and knowledge about motives and attitudes of the speaker.

Human beings learn language spontaneously and, barring extreme cases, it does not depend on level of intelligence. The approximate chronology of development is outlined below.

Language development from infancy

▶ *Birth* – The left hemisphere of the brain tends to be the one predominantly involved in language processing. Some psychologists believe this specialisation begins around the age of about five, but others believe it is present at birth. It would seem that at least the programme for hemispherical specialisation must be present at birth.

▶ *6-9 months* – Babbling occurs. This sounds a bit like speech as it seems to have the same kind of intonational quality.

▶ *9-10 months* – Babbling starts to become contracted into recognisable phones of the native tongue of its parents.

▶ *12 months* – First word spoken.

▶ *13-19 months* – Vocabulary of about ten words. After this the list increases rapidly. Single word sentences are still used.

Nelson analysed the first fifty words a child learns. His analysis is as follows:[4]

Type of word	Percentage of total
specific nominals	14
general	51
action words	13
modifiers	9
personal-social words	8
function words	4

A child's earliest uttered words are context bound. In other words, they only have meaning in a particular context.[5] A child may learn to refer to a car outside its window by the term car. It would not follow that it would refer to a car anywhere else by that name. New words tend to be acquired in a context bound way and gradually the child learns to decontextualise them.

► *Eighteen months* – Telegraphic speech: from here, children begin to use two-word communications. **Connectives** begin to be used to link the words together, but **functors** such as the words *is* and *are* are omitted.[6] Communications continue to be supported by gestures and context and adults continue to simplify the language they use to communicate with their infants.

► *Twenty-four months* – By two years of age infants know quite a lot of words.

► *Thirty months* – Stage two grammar begins at around thirty months. Most English-speaking children have mastered twenty-seven of the language's forty phonemes.

► *Four years* – Children still have trouble with at least one phoneme of a language, but have mastered basic grammar[7] (everything except the passive voice and irregular words).

► *6-7 years* – The child speaks more or less as well as an adult does, except that it still has difficulty with the passive voice.[7]

▶ *Seven years* — All the phonemes are mastered.

▶ *10-11 years* — This is a critical period for language development.[8]

Case study

It seems that it is possible to learn more or less from scratch very close to this critical period. Ten year old Alex Oliver underwent a left hemispherectomy (removal of the left hemisphere) at Great Ormond Street Hospital Institute of Child Health in 1997. It was an attempt to cure epilepsy. Up to this time he could not speak, but since the operation has made rapid progress in this respect. Not only does this show that language can be learnt right up to the critical period, but also that the left hemisphere is not crucial to language development. It seems, in this case, that the faulty left hemisphere, being naturally the one responsible for language processing, was preventing the right hemisphere taking over the job which the left hemisphere could not manage. Once the left hemisphere was out of the way, the right hemisphere could take over the job unhindered.

There is evidence that children can develop substantial language ability after the critical period, but they never reach levels of normality.[9]

Taking a behaviourist approach

Behaviourists explain language development in terms of:

▶ imitation
▶ reinforcement
▶ shaping.

Learning by imitation

Parents encourage infants to copy their words. To help them, they speak to them in quasi baby language, reducing the complexity of their adult speech.

Reinforcement

When a child repeats a word its parents say to it, the joy and excitement it sees on their faces reinforces the production of the word.

▶ *Reinforcing grammar* – Skinner argued that parents reinforce correct grammar usage.[10] This has been challenged.[11,12,13]

▶ *Learning by reinforcement* – Children gradually learn that they can use language to obtain what they want. Adults reinforce language by giving them what they want, or helping them get it. The primary motivation for language acquisition becomes instrumental.[14,15]

Shaping
Early in a child's development adults help them understand the value of language by attributing meanings to their pre-linguistic sounds and gestures.[16]

Language Acquisition Support System (LASS)
Adults also teach children turn-taking,[15] help them understand how to express commands, and teach them how to ask and answer questions. Such common response to the developmental needs of children is known as the *Language Acquisition Support System (LASS)*.

Weaknesses of behaviourist theories
Behaviourist theories cannot explain:

▶ creativity in language use
▶ unlearned grammar
▶ the universal consistency of the order of stages of language development
▶ comprehension of the meaning of sentences.

Taking a psychobiological approach

Chomsky and Lenneberg are convinced that language is a uniquely human attribute. Biologically, we have evolved to communicate in this complex way. Our vocal chords, our auditory system, our breathing and our cerebrum are all uniquely appropriate for this form of communication. To bring it out, however, interaction with other people is important.

Development of surface grammar

Children seem to naturally develop grammar.[17] They do this on their own. This can be seen by observing the mistakes they make. Sometimes they stick rigidly to a rule when it is not conventional to do so. They will typically add an 's' to all words to be pluralised, even if it is conventional not to do so, as with the words fish and sheep. Parents are usually not concerned about grammar. In fact, their own is often faulty.[17]

Biological changes

Our development from infant babble to words is accompanied by physiological changes in the cerebrum and hemispherical specialisation for language use tends to take place at around five years of age. From that point on, the left hemisphere becomes dominant for language use. The right hemisphere can take over the function if the left is faulty, but only by complete surgical removal of the latter will it be able to do so.

Testing the nature/nurture question

It is not very defensible to say that all forms of language are unique to humans. Researchers have been teaching it to apes, using sign language, with a good deal of success.[18,19,20,21]

Taking a cognitive approach

It has been argued that before language can be learned cognitive structures (such as cause and effect sequences) must develop. They come first, then language develops to talk about them.[22]

Chomsky's theory of innate language ability

The key elements of Chomsky's theory are:

► a universal grammar
► linguistic universals
► a language acquisition device (LAD).

Linguistic universals

Some things are common to all languages. Chomsky calls these 'linguistic universals'. They include:

consonants	subjects
vowels	verbs
syllables	predicates
epithets	modifiers
nouns	objects

Language Acquisition Device (LAD)

Chomsky argued that human beings have a language acquisition device comprising:

▶ a hypothesis-making mechanism
▶ transformational grammar.

Transformational grammar

Transformational grammar is the structural rule by which we derive meaning from language. Chomsky argued that this is innate rather than learned, and that it is a universal characteristic of human beings.

These devices do not depend on speech, for they are evident in the development of deaf children too.

Chomsky argued that the language acquisition device seems to be independent of other cognitive abilities.

Tutorial

Practice questions

1. List Hocket's thirteen design features of language.

2. Name two fundamental elements of language.

3. In psycholinguistics 'phones' are:

    ☐ groups of sounds with a common meaning
    ☐ devices to call your friends on
    ☐ individual sounds of the most basic nature

    Tick the correct answer.

4. What is morphology?

5. What is syntax?

6. How do adults reinforce correct language in children?

Seminar discussion
Is language a peculiarly human ability?

Practical assignment
Ask the mothers of half a dozen of your friends the ages at which your friends began to babble, form their first word, utter their first pair of words and so on. Compare their answers with the empirical norms given on pages 95 to 97.

Course work, revision and exam tips
You can enhance the storage and recall of your memory many-fold by using appropriate memory techniques. Such techniques take the drudgery out of revision and make 100% recall of key facts quite attainable. Readers can quickly grasp proven skills for this from my book *Maximising Your Memory*, full details of which are given in the Further Reading section at the end of this book.

Bibliographical notes

1   Hocket 1960
2   Aitchison 1983
3   Chomsky 1957
4   Nelson 1973
5   Barrett 1986
6   Brown 1965
7   Milner 1951
8   Lenneberg 1967
9   Skuse 1984
10 Skinner 1957
11 Brown *et al.* 1969
12 Braine 1971
13 Tizard *et al.* 1972
14 Bates *et al.* 1979
15 Bruner 1983
16 Snow 1977
17 Slobin 1975
18 Gardner and Gardner 1969
19 Premack 1971
20 Savage and Rumbaugh *et al.* 1980
21 Patterson 1980
22 Cromer 1974

10

Adolescence

One minute summary — Adolescence is often thought to be a difficult time, but there is evidence that most young people cope with it without difficulty. Focal theory explains how adolescents cope with adolescence by staggering the transitions they have to make. Freud and Erikson are the two main theorists on adolescence. Adolescence is a time for important transitions, but it is not the last chance for them to occur. Physical changes take place in adolescence. Adolescents tend to be prone to low self-esteem. A person's socio-cultural context will influence their experience of adolescence. Adolescence is one of the times when the psyche is in a state of flux and, therefore, malleable. Two new defence mechanisms arise. The special conflicts of adolescence resemble earlier conflicts in childhood.

In this chapter you will learn about:

▶ the nature of adolescence
▶ the cognitive view
▶ the psychoanalytical view
▶ the psychobiological view
▶ the view of social psychologists
▶ the humanist view.

Learning objectives

Once you have finished this chapter you should:

1. know what contributions to understanding adolescence are made by each of the main schools of thought. You should then be able to tackle questions on adolescence from different psychological viewpoints.

2. know the main theories and models of adolescence.

Defining adolescence

Adolescence is a stage of development falling roughly between the ages of 12 and 25. This phase of life contains its own special problems. Hall *et al* described it as a period of storm and stress.[1]

Most find no problem

Not all authorities share Hall's view. Evidence shows that most adolescents adjust well and find no great difficulty at this stage in their lives. They cope well with:[4,9]

- ▶ the task of **individuation**
- ▶ the severing of attachments to parents
- ▶ decisions about their future.

Some studies have found that adolescents generally feel psychologically independent from their parents by 13 or 14 years of age.[3]

Taking a cognitive approach

The focal theory of attention

Coleman's 'focal theory of attention' explains how most adolescents manage the transition without difficulty. They do it by staggering the changes. The ones who find adolescence a time of storm and stress tend to be the ones who try to do it all at once. Coleman's data has been replicated and the same results have been found from data from other countries.

Adolescence is characterised by:

- ▶ mood swings
- ▶ egocentricity
- ▶ challenge to conventional thinking
- ▶ ambivalence.

Development of self
Adolescence is a time when important developments are taking place in individual's self-concepts, through a process of adaptation to their new situations. This adaptation includes:

▶ severing of childhood type relationship with parents
▶ coming to terms with their new identity
▶ facing up to their future responsibilities as adults.

Taking a psychoanalytical approach

Psychoanalysts see the main problem for adolescents as the development of ego identity, a clear sense of who they are, where they come from, and where they are going. This is what is known as **individuation**.

A psychological state of flux
There are points in life where the forces acting upon an individual's psychological stability are so strong that they put it in a state of flux. These forces include conflicts, fears and uncertainties. At this point their ego identity is malleable. Its direction can change, like a turntable whose restraining brakes have been loosened.

Once that pivotal stage of life has passed, the doubts, fears, conflicts and the significance attached to it by the self and others are no longer in mind the structures of the ego once again gel into a degree of rigidity. Adolescence is one such time.

Elements of the state of flux
The state of flux, or identity confusion in which adolescents find themselves can be described in terms of four elements:

▶ *intimacy* – adolescents fear that intimacy presents a threat to their identity.

▶ *anxiety* – anxiety about the future leads to avoidance of thought about it.

▶ *direction* – adolescents find difficulty in applying themselves to goals.

▶ *identity* – uncertainty about identity can lead to acceptance of negative identity, as better than no identity at all.

Inner conflicts are reminiscent of old conflicts
The kind of conflicts an adolescent experiences in this stage of their life are reminiscent of conflicts at earlier developmental stages – they all involve conflict with authority figures.

Adolescent defence mechanisms
Two new defence mechanisms appear in adolescence:[12]

▶ intellectualisation
▶ asceticism.

The defence mechanisms which developed prior to this stage of development prove inadequate for the increased levels of feeling experienced in adolescence.

Intimacy and sexual identity
The adolescent becomes aware of significant sexual feelings and has to choose a sexual identity. Without making such choice they will be unable to achieve intimacy.

Adolescence is the ideal time for choosing one's sexual identity.[8] A selection too early can lead to problems later on. It is not uncommon for people who are married with children to leave their partner for a partner of their own sex. Sexual identity choices were likely to have been made too early with pressure, however subtle, from others.

Adolescence is not the 'Last Chance Saloon'
Although adolescence is the ideal time to make such choices, it is not absolutely crucial. Change can be made at various points throughout life. Erikson mapped out eight stages, each separated by a crisis period, when the ego will become malleable. That is not to say that change cannot take place between the crises, but it is less likely.[8]

Taking a psychobiological approach

Physical growth, changes in body shape, the growth of body hair in new places, change in voice quality and various other things give adolescents reason to feel they do not have the control over their body which they once felt they had. They also experience mood swings and strong sexual desires.

Taking a social psychological approach

Importance of others

The severance of the relationship with parents leaves a void. Adolescents try to compensate for this in a number of ways, seeking[13]

- ▶ exciting experiences
- ▶ group experiences
- ▶ changing relationships and
- ▶ modelling on hero figures.

Young people's work plays an important role in the formation of their identity. To lose a job has important psychological consequences.[6,7,8]

Cultural relativism

Adolescence cannot be understood in isolation from its cultural context. This approach is known as cultural relativism. Social factors have an impact on the adolescent.[5] Some of the issues with which adolescents have to cope are:

- ▶ attitude towards parents
- ▶ conformity to parental wishes
- ▶ values
- ▶ social class
- ▶ morality
- ▶ gender roles.

The culture in which an individual is brought up will influence the way they respond to these challenges.[5] Some societies are more family orientated than others. For some, the degree of conformity will extend to allowing their parents to choose their marriage partners. In others, the level of rejection of parental influence will often be quite considerable.

Taking a humanist approach

Some authorities[14] have argued that adolescence is characterised by low self-esteem and unstable self-concept, with females affected most. Others[15] have produced data which challenge this, however. Furthermore, the former findings were based on pre-1975 data. A lot may have changed in gender terms since then.

Tutorial

Practice questions

1. State one model that derives from the cognitive perspective on adolescence.

2. What do psychoanalysts see as the main problem of adolescence?

3. What does the social psychology perspective contribute to our knowledge?

4. What knowledge can be said to derive from the humanist perspective?

5. Name four elements of the state of flux that Erikson referred to.

6. Name two new defence mechanisms which psychoanalysts say appear in adolescence.

Seminar discussion
How useful is the concept of adolescence?

Practical assignment

Ask three adults to describe how they experienced adolescence. If possible select from different generations, and/or cultures.

Course work, revision and exam tips

When approaching the exams, plan your revision timetable carefully to ensure you give adequate time to each subject. Don't rely on cramming — it doesn't work.

Bibliographical notes

[1] Hall 1904
[2] Rutter *et al.* 1976
[3] Bandura 1972
[4] See also Siddique and D'Arcy 1984
[5] Mead 1961
[6] Merton 1968
[7] Kelvin 1981
[8] Erikson 1968
[9] Offer 1969
[12] Coleman 1980
[12] Freud (Anna) 1937
[13] Blos 1967
[14] Simmons and Rosenberg 1975
[15] Coleman and Hendry 1990

Adulthood

One minute summary – Adulthood is distinguished from adolescence by the fact that the individuals concerned have, ideally, accepted their freedom of action, and responsibility for the outcomes. Individuals tend to develop through adulthood by way of a reasonably common set of transitions. Levinson and Gould are the two most prominent writers on adulthood. The way individuals experience adulthood depends on their socio-cultural context. A capacity for intimacy is important in adulthood.

In this chapter you will learn about:

▶ the nature of adulthood
▶ empirical knowledge of adulthood
▶ the social psychology of adulthood.

Learning objectives

Once you have finished this chapter you should know:

1. what contributions to understanding adulthood are made by each of the main schools of thought. You should then be able to deal successfully with questions on adulthood from several psychological viewpoints.

2. the main theories and models of adulthood.

Defining adulthood

Adulthood is the stage of development falling roughly between the ages of 25 and 65. It is the stage where we admit to ourselves that we

must put aside the illusions of childhood and accept that there are
no certainties as we had once believed. Our survival is now up to us.
In adulthood we accept that we are free to make up our own minds,
but must accept responsibility for our actions and their consequences.

The adult role
Adults must:

▶ accept social roles
▶ take responsibility
▶ empathise with others
▶ make decisions
▶ cope with problems.

How adults differ from children and adolescents
We distinguish adults from children and adolescents by the adult's:

▶ clear value systems
▶ emotional stability
▶ intellectual insight
▶ realistic aims
▶ realistic self concept
▶ strong positive social relationships
▶ ability for intimacy.

Empirical knowledge of adulthood

From a survey of 500 individuals, Gould found that the following
chronology describes the experience of adulthood for most people.[1]

Twenties
The individual is aware that they are free to do as they wish, and
think what they choose, but they do not yet exercise their total
freedom. They realise there are advantages in letting their parents
still have a say.

End of twenties/beginning of thirties
A sense of the finiteness of the human lifespan develops. Individuals are forced to make choices on how they will spend their future years.

Thirty-five to forty-five
In this stage, individuals have usually completed the transition to full acceptance of responsibility for their own thoughts and actions. No longer do they surrender any of their freedom of will to their parents. They become aware of how quickly time slips away and this preoccupation remains with them from here on. This all represents a significant shift in the way individuals view the world and themselves. If they do not make this transition they will be likely to see their life as meaningless and tend to despair.

Thirty to fifty
By now, individuals have completely thrown off their illusions of safety in the world. They know they must stand on their own feet.[1]

Levinson's seasons of life
Levinson *et al* identified nine stages in adult life:[2]

Stage one: 17 to 22 years
The individual separates from parents and childhood and attaches to the adult world.

Stage two: 22 to 28 years (early structuring stage)
Here, the individual strikes a balance between making commitments and keeping options open. This refers to various aspects of their lives, including their relationship with their partner, their friends, their job, their values and their way of life.

Stage three: 28 to 33 years
This is a time where self doubt is strong. The awareness that time is slipping away is present. There is a sense that if the individual is going to change their direction they have to change now. An identity crisis around the age of 30 is common.

Stage four: 33 to 40 years
This can be regarded as the settling down stage. There are two sub-stages:

▶ nest building
▶ goal achievement.

Mentoring younger friends is not uncommon in this stage of life.

Stage five: 40 to 45 years
This stage is sometimes referred to as the mid-life transition. In it, old life structures are ended and new ones embarked upon. The lifelong central aim of individuation continues. There is soul searching, but increased confidence. For some, this transitional stage is easy, but for others it is more problematic and slow.

Stage six: 45 to 50 years
By this time of life, the commitment to what is worthwhile and what is not has normally been made. Choices of new life structures often have to be made, sometimes as a result of divorce, illness, or bereavement.

Stage seven: 50 to 55 years
If a mid-life crisis was not experienced in stage 5 an individual will be likely to have one during this stage.[2]

Stage eight: 55 to 60 years
An individual's life structure is now quite firmly established and the settling down period begins.

Stage nine: 60 to 65 years
This is often referred to as the late adult transition. It leads up to retirement.

A major weakness of Levinson's work is that it was based on small-scale data, biased in terms of sex and occupation. The sample size was only 40 compared with Gould's sample of 500.

Do people really conform to a pattern?
Is it plausible that people conform to a pattern? Aren't individuals all unique? Some researchers have claimed they are.[3] However, there are some very observable constancies among human beings. They include biological changes, for example. There are differences

in people's rate of biological ageing, but there is also a high degree of consistency between human beings in this respect.

In addition, the conditions which make demands on peoples' lives tend to change in predicable ways at predictable stages in their lives. One example is children growing up and leaving home. These conditions have unusual effects upon the hitherto continuous way of life. It is not hard to see, therefore, why crises occur at predictable age ranges among individuals in general in the western world. However, there will always be those who deviate from the norm.[4]

Social psychology of adulthood

We are all influenced in our actions and thoughts by the expectations of others. This may, indeed, be why people choose their own age group to associate with. It gives them norms. People tend to judge whether their rate of change is normal by reference to others.

Tutorial

Practice questions

1. What contribution to the psychology of adulthood derives from the social psychology perspective?

2. What contribution to the psychology of adulthood derives from a psychoanalytical perspective?

3. State seven ways in which adults can be distinguished from children and adolescence.

4. List Levinson et al's 'seasons of life'.

5. How useful is chronological age compared with biological or psychological age?

6. How far do people conform to a pattern of development in adulthood?

Seminar discussion
To what extent do people conform to the norms of their age group?

Practical assignment
Ask a middle-aged adult what was important at various stages in their life. State the age parameters of Levinson's stages, but don't give details of what you expect them to say, otherwise they may try to conform to your expectations. Compare the data you have generated with Levinson's theory.

Course work, revision and exam tips
Handling exam anxiety
Revise up to the night before, for morning exams, and to lunchtime, for afternoon exams. In the latter case give yourself at least two and a half hours before the exam to switch off. Get to the centre early. There's nothing worse for stress than being caught in traffic holdups close to the scheduled exam time.

Outside the exam room, stay away from those who are showing signs of stress – it's catching. Don't think about the subject. Keep your mind cool until you get into the exam room and are told to start.

Bibliographical notes
[1]   Gould 1978
[2]   Levinson *et al.* 1978
[3]   Hobson and Scally 1980
[4]   Fiske 1984

12

Ageing

One minute summary – There are different concepts of ageing. Erikson argued that the main challenge for the aged is coming to terms with impending death. The personal growth model is a prescriptive model, which states how people ought to deal with old age, to achieve maximum fulfilment and least despair. Fluid intelligence and short-term memory deteriorate slightly, but long-term memory does not. Crystallised intelligence goes on increasing into the 80s. Social exchange theory sees old age as a time when we lose the advantage of some roles, but gain others in exchange. Social disengagement theory suggests that those old people who disengage themselves from society are isolationist. Activity theory suggests that the aged should seek to maintain their role count. The decrement model sees old age in terms of decline and decay.

In this chapter you will learn about:

▶ concepts of age
▶ the psychoanalytical approach to ageing
▶ the cognitive approach to ageing
▶ the psychobiological approach to ageing
▶ the humanist approach to ageing
▶ the social psychological approach to ageing.

Learning objectives

Once you have finished this chapter you should:

1. know what contributions to understanding of ageing are made by each of the main schools of thought

2. be able successfully to tackle questions on ageing from the different psychological perspectives

3.　know the main theories and models of ageing.

Ideas about ageing

The post 65 year period of human life is of interest to most of the major sub-disciplines in psychology.

Significant differences in physical and mental maturity are found between one individual and another. People differ in both their outlooks and their self perceptions. Some young people are psychologically old before their time and there are old people who are still young at heart.

Concepts of age

The value of simple chronology as a measure of age is that it does not vary. Ten people born on the same date will all age chronologically at exactly the same rate. Chronological age provides us with an easy way of classifying people according to their expected behaviour and development. Although there are significant variations in physiological and psychological development, there are statistical norms for each age group (see pages 110–112). Chronological ages, therefore, enable us to make our social world predictable.

Different measures of age

We can identify several different kinds of age:

▶ chronological age
▶ biological age
▶ subjective age
▶ functional age
▶ mental maturity.

Taking a psychoanalytical approach

Erikson has provided the main contribution to the literature on the psychology of ageing. The main task for the aged is to come to terms with their impending death.[1] Old age is yet another crisis period in life. There are two ways the individual can go. They can focus on despair, or focus on the continuing development of their ego integrity. The crisis cannot be avoided; it has to be faced. The challenge, Erikson argues, is to reach the end of their lives with more integrity than despair.[11]

Ambivalence towards death

Old people tend to exhibit ambivalence in handling the issue of their impending death. Some of the time they wish to avoid thinking about it; at other times they want to talk about it.

Taking a social psychological approach

Social psychology is concerned with:

1. psychological effects of social behaviour
2. social effects of psychological behaviour.

Social psychology provides three important models of social interaction in old age:

▶ social exchange theory
▶ social disengagement theory
▶ activity theory.

Social exchange theory

Social exchange theory suggests that old age should be seen as a time when some role advantages have to be relinquished, but they are replaced by opportunities for others. Previously, the individual played an active economic role in society. Now he or she relinquishes that role in exchange for freedom from responsibility and increased leisure time.[4]

Social disengagement theory

Social disengagement theory[5] provides that some old people tend to isolate themselves from their social world. Such individuals would probably have isolated themselves to some extent when they were younger, too.

Activity theory

Activity theory[6,7] assumes that it is not the individual who disengages from society, but society that disengages from the individual. Negative attitudes to ageing prevail in western society. As a result, older people become discriminated against at work, and tend to be shunned by members of their families. This has a negative effect on how they see themselves, and this in turn affects their behaviour. Anti-social behaviour will, in turn, reinforce a negative attitude of younger members of society towards them.

Activity theory holds that the natural tendency of old people is affiliative. They want to engage with people of younger age. The theory is prescriptive. It argues that, to deflect the sources of disengagement, old people should seek to maintain their role count. Old age takes away some social roles, but it provides opportunities for others.

Bereavement

There are much more tangible social factors which negatively affect old people's quality of life. For example, old people are more likely to suffer bereavement than younger people. Bereavement has its own developmental stages:

- ▶ shock/disbelief
- ▶ awareness
- ▶ resolution.

Taking a cognitive approach

Neural activity

Neural activity in old people slows down. Neural signals in eighty year olds are between 15% and 20% slower than they are in twenty year olds.[12] This could account for the decrease in 'fluid intelligence' which tends to be found. One explanation of differences in intelligence between individuals is differences in neural speed.

The changes in intelligence, however, are not negative overall. While fluid intelligence continues the decline it started earlier in life, crystallised intelligence (the kind which derives from schemata formation) goes on increasing until at least into the 80s.[3] This type of intelligence is arguably the more important.

Memory
Short-term memory tends to deteriorate to some degree. This is most noticeable where tasks are particularly demanding of close attention. Co-ordination between the functioning of long and short-term memory also appears to decline.

Taking a psychobiological approach

Male and female menopause symptoms
Females undergo a physiological menopause. It is often argued that men experience some kind of male counterpart. The female menopause tends to be associated with certain negative psychological effects – for example, insomnia and depression. The menopause, however, often begins before old age.

Cell senescence
Brain cell **senescence** (brain cell death) is an ongoing process. When it reaches a particular stage **dementia** occurs. Dementia manifests itself in:

- severe memory loss
- states of confusion
- frustration.

   Closely allied to this, in terms of symptoms, are Alzheimer's disease and Pick's disease. Both predominantly affect old people, though they can sometimes be found in younger people. Alzheimer's disease and Pick's disease produce identical symptoms. The only way they can be distinguished is by post mortem examination.

Taking a humanist approach

The quality of life of old people depends partly on how old they perceive themselves. Remember, chronological age is not the only measure of age. Kastenbaum devised a questionnaire to test how old people perceived themselves to be.[9]

Decrement model
Some people think of growing old as a process of decline and decay. This is not the only way to look at it, though.

Personal growth model
An alternative, and much more positive, way of thinking of old age is this. For the first time in their lives, most old people are free of their everyday responsibilities. Such things as going to work and looking after the children will have limited their freedom to do all the things they would have liked to have done when they were younger. Now, in old age, those responsibilities aren't there. Furthermore, for many, the money to do such things is now available, when it was not so before.

While the resources and time are available for them to fulfil their dreams, old people are aware that there is no time to waste on trivia. They are motivated therefore to get on with doing what they see as important to them.[10]

Tutorial

Practice questions

1. What contribution does cognitive psychology make to the study of old age?

2. What contribution does social psychology make to the study of old age?

3. What contribution does psychobiology make to the study of old age?

4. What contribution does humanist psychology make to the study of old age?

5. What is the main task of old age according to Erikson's psycho-social theory?

6. State three cognitive changes that occur in old age.

Seminar discussion
How useful is the concept of chronological age?

Practical assignment
Interview an old person, asking them about their quality of life, including whether or not they feel isolated from other age groups. Ask yourself which theories fit the data you generate.

Course work, revision and exam tips
On the day of your exams once you are inside the exam room and told to start, read the questions carefully. Don't rush to start and don't be alarmed if other people are already writing while you are still preparing. You may well notice them later sitting with their pencils in their mouths, lost for ideas, while you are writing incessantly.

Bibliographical notes

[1] Peck 1968
[2] Botwinick 1978
[3] Nesselroade et al. 1972
[4] Dowd 1975
[5] Cummings and Henry 1961
[6] Havinghurst 1964
[7] Maddox 1964
[8] Engel 1962
[9] Kastenbaum 1974
[10] Kalish 1982
[11] Erikson 1980
[12] Bee and Mitchell 1980

13

Moral Development

One minute summary – The three principal aspects of moral behaviour are: behavioural, cognitive and affective. The doctrine of specificity holds that moral standards observed are specific to situations. Behaviourists explain moral behaviour in terms of reward and punishment. Psychoanalysts explain it in terms of development of the superego. Social learning theorists explain it in terms of observed rewards and punishment bestowed on a model. Cognitive psychologists explain it in terms of providing a rationale.

In this chapter you will learn how moral development is explained from the following perspectives:

▶ behaviourist
▶ psychoanalytical
▶ cognitive
▶ psychobiological
▶ humanist
▶ social psychological.

Learning objectives

By the time you have finished this chapter you should:

1. know what each main school of thought has contributed to our understanding of moral development

2. be able to successfully tackle questions on moral development from different psychological perspectives

3. know the main theories and models of moral development.

Moral behaviour

Moral behaviour has three components:

1. behavioural
2. cognitive
3. affective.

Doctrine of specificity

People's moral standards do not appear to be consistent across different situations. Even in similar situations consistency is rather low (correlation 0.34).

▶ *Key point* – Moral behaviour is determined by both situation and personality.[1]

Taking a behaviourist approach

When individuals do something they believe is wrong they experience a guilty conscience. To behaviourists, the guilty conscience is merely the accumulated associations between that behaviour and its consequence in terms of punishment. The term they use is a **conditioned emotional response** (CER).

It has been argued that punishment leads to feelings of guilt following a wrongful act, more than an actual inhibition to perform it. If punishment were given immediately *before* a wrongful act, then an individual would accumulate mental associations between the intentions to perform the act, and the punishment that would follow.[2]

People do develop inhibitions, despite the absence of obvious punishment for their intention. It may be because they work out the consequences of the act.

Furthermore, although it is not feasible to administer physical punishment in anticipation of a wrongful act, something similar can be done. A strong threatening warning can cause acute discomfort for the individual, in the form of anxiety.

Negative effects of punishment

There are two ways that punishment can have a negative effect:

1. It can perpetuate wrongful behaviour and, perhaps, make it even more likely. A punisher provides a role model to the victim. It is an aggressive and oppressive model, which seeks to bend others to its will by violent means. The model is also one who assumes that their rights and values come above those of other people.

2. Another way that punishment can have negative effects on the morality of people's behaviour is that it produces anger and resentment. If this is stored up it may eventually become too great for the person to contain. The result may be aggressive action against the punishers, or even against people who have had no part in administering the punishment.

Methods of punishment

A distinction can be made between physical and psychological methods of punishment.

▶ Physical methods include such things as beatings, groundings and curfews.

▶ Psychological methods include such practices as withdrawal of shows of love and approval.

Psychological methods are found to be the most effective.[3,4,5,17]

Sometimes punishment is given together with humiliation. Centuries ago, people were put in the stocks or the pillory, where other people would throw things at them.

Public punishment is less effective than private punishment. It may, however, serve a wider purpose of providing a warning to others contemplating similar wrongdoings. It may, therefore, serve a dual purpose of instilling guilt into the actual wrongdoer and inhibition into potential wrongdoers.

Reward

Reward serves the opposite function of punishment. While punishment seeks to prevent immoral behaviour, reward seeks to encourage moral behaviour. The process works in the same way. The subconscious mind associates positive feelings with particular acts.

The paradox of reward

The function of reward is not straightforward. Some behaviours are intrinsically rewarding, that is they are enjoyable in themselves. Entertaining an audience by playing a musical instrument, is one example. Other behaviours may be performed because of an extrinsic reward. Undesirable, but highly paid, work is an example.

The complication arises when an extrinsic reward is given for behaviour which is intrinsically rewarding. When this happens, individuals replace their original reason for performing the behaviour – an expectation of intrinsic reward – with a new rationale of expectation of an extrinsic reward. If the extrinsic reward is later removed the motivation to perform that behaviour will decrease. This is known as the 'paradox of reward'.[5,6]

This, of course, has implications for anyone who does something they enjoy for a living.

Combination of punishment and reward

Punishment and reward are found to be more effective together than punishment alone.[7]

Punishment as reward

The worst kind of punishment is being ignored. Even active punishment of a physical or psychological nature is preferable to being ignored altogether.

Taking a psychoanalytical approach

Freud's theory of moral development contains two main components:

1. guilt
2. pride.

These are the products of the **conscience** and the **ego ideal** respectively. When we do something we consider morally wrong our conscience makes us feel guilt. When we do something we believe is morally right our ego ideal gives us a sense of pride.

Level of moral behaviour and level of guilt are inversely related. If we stifle our desire for immoral behaviour the energy which fuels the desire must go somewhere. It may go to fuel the feeling of guilt.

Freud, however, argued that desire for wrongdoing and guilt are not directly proportional.

Timing of development of the conscience

Freud argued that the conscience develops in childhood. Others, however, argue that moral development goes on throughout life.[14,15]

In Freudian theory the phallic stage of development is particularly important. This is where male children experience the Oedipus complex and females the Electra complex, both resulting in identification with their same sex parent.

Freud's theory would suggest that males identify more strongly with their fathers than females do with their mothers during the phallic stage, because of the greater fear involved – fear of castration. It might be expected, therefore, that males would develop stronger consciences than females. Freud believed this was so.

Some of Freud's theory, however, tends to be regarded as out of date now. After all, times have changed. Patterns of child rearing are very different from what they were in Freud's time. Freud believed the conscience was rooted in family interaction. Today, children have many influences from authority figures outside the family.

Taking a social learning theory approach

Social learning theory is an attempt to combine social psychology with behaviourist psychology. Rather than the individuals being rewarded, or punished directly, they observe **role models** being rewarded or punished for particular behaviours, and so they copy or avoid such behaviour. The principal authority in this area of knowledge is Bandura.

A role model's effectiveness depends on the following:

▶ appropriateness
▶ consistency of behaviour
▶ friendliness
▶ observed punishment
▶ observed rewards

▶ powerfulness
▶ relevance.

Taking a cognitive approach

Providing a rationale

The reforming effect is particularly good when punishment is accompanied by reasons for refraining from wrongful acts.[16] Moreover, when reasons are given the timing of punishment appears to lose its importance.

The type of rationale that will work is age-related. Owner-related explanations, such as:

'You can't have that. It belongs to Barry.'

are not likely to work with very young infants. However, object-related explanations can be effective[19] for example:

'Don't touch that. You'll break it.'

Tutorial

Practice questions

1. To what extent are Freud's theories still relevant?

2. How can society constructively use what we now know about moral development?

3. How useful is social learning theory?

4. What factors determine a model's effectiveness?

5. What punishments work best?

☐ Physical
☐ Psychological

Tick the correct box.

Seminar discussion
To what extent can we excuse immoral behaviour and to what extent should we blame people for it?

Practial asssignment
Consider whether Freud's theory of moral development is still appropriate or whether it is outdated. Give your reasons.

Course work, revision and exam tips
Allocate a specific amount of time for each essay question and stick to it. If you are being asked to answer four questions don't think of doing three questions well rather than four less well. The strategy won't work. Pick out the questions you intend to do and one extra for good measure. Brainstorm for about four minutes per subject. This means just jotting down everything that seems in any way relevant. Don't discriminate, or evaluate the ideas, just jot them down, discrimination and evaluation come later.

Bibliographical notes

[1] Hartshorne and May 1930
[2] Aronfreed 1963
[3] Sears, Maccoby and Levin 1957
[4] Hoffman 1970
[5] Bem 1972
[6] Lepper and Greene 1978
[7] Perry and Parke 1975
[8] Danziger 1971
[9] Glueck and Glueck 1950
[10] Bandura and Walters 1959
[11] Kohlberg 1969
[12] Hoffman 1976
[13] Bandura et al. 1961
[14] Parke 1972
[15] Parke 1977
[16] Parke 1974
[17] Mackinnon 1938

14

The Brain and Nervous System

One minute summary – The main parts of the brain are the forebrain, midbrain and hindbrain. The forebrain is made up of the two hemispheres of the cerebrum. The upper part of the cerebrum is a folded layer known as the cortex. The midbrain plays an important role in consciousness. The hindbrain contains the cerebellum, the pons and the medulla oblongata. The spinal cord connects the brain to the peripheral nervous system. The peripheral nervous system has two parts: the sympathetic branch (which prepares the body for action) and the parasympathetic branch (which prepares it for rest).

In this chapter you will learn about:

▶ the brain
▶ the spinal cord
▶ neurons.

Learning objectives

Once you have finished this chapter you should:

1. Know some of the main structures of the brain and nervous system.

2. Understand basically how they work.

3. Know something of the functions they fulfil.

The brain

The biological basis of the mind is the brain and the central nervous system. The main parts of the brain are the:

▶ cortex
▶ forebrain
▶ midbrain
▶ hindbrain.

The cerebrum

There are two hemispheres of the cerebrum. They appear identical, although they become configured differently early in life to play different roles. The different sections of the cerebrum are referred to as *lobes*. They are the:

▶ frontal lobe
▶ parietal lobe
▶ temporal lobe
▶ occipital lobe.

The cortex

There are three important principles by which the cortex functions. They are:

▶ *The law of equipotentiality* – provides that if there is damage to one hemisphere the corresponding areas of the other hemisphere take over the roles that are concerned.

▶ *The law of mass action*[1]– provides that it is not the location of brain damage that is important for functioning, it is the amount.

▶ *The principle of multiple control* – provides that each part of the brain carries out not one, but several functions.

Motor behaviour

Motor behaviour refers to physical movement. It is controlled by two strips, one each side of the fissure of Rolando (see below).

1. The strip at the front of the fissure controls outgoing signals, that is those passing from the brain to the body.

2. The strip behind the fissure controls feedback from the body.

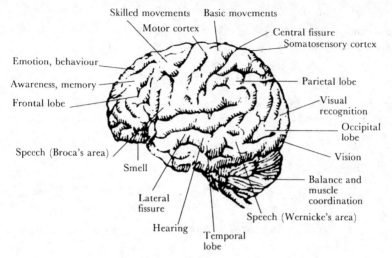

Figure 4. The parts of the brain and their functions.

The left side of the body is controlled by the right side of the brain and vice versa. Consequently, the neural pathways must cross over. This is known as **corticospinal decussation** and takes place in a sub-cortical structure known as the medulla.

Forebrain
The forebrain consists of the two cerebral hemispheres. The top layer is known as the cortex. It consists of about two and a half square metres of folded neural tissue, about 1 cm thick. The folds in the cortex lie along two paths:

► the fissure of Rolando
► the fissure of Sylvius.

The fissure of Rolando is a vertical fissure; it separates the frontal lobe and the parietal lobe in each hemisphere. The fissure of Sylvius runs laterally, separating the frontal lobe from the temporal lobe.

The limbic system
The two hemispheres of the brain are connected via the **corpus callosum.** Below this lie a number of structures collectively referred to as the **limbic system.** They are the:

- thalamus
- hypothalamus
- mamillary body
- cingulate gyrus
- hippocampus
- amygdala
- fornix
- olfactory bulb.

The thalamus

The thalamus refers to two grey, egg-shaped bodies. Like other brain structures, the thalamus plays a number of roles. These are:

(a) relaying information from the ears, eyes and body to the cortex
(b) consciousness regulation.

The hypothalamus

This is a small structure, a little under half an inch in diameter. It plays a key role in motivation and **homeostasis** (maintaining stability in the various aspects of the body's internal environment).

The hypothalamus has several sub-parts and each of them has a special role to play:

Sub part	Role
anterior	water balance
super optic	" "
posterior	sex drive
pre-super optic	heat
ventromedial	hunger
dorsomedial	aggression
dorsal	pleasure

Basal ganglia

This structure comprises three sub-structures:

(a) amygdala
(b) corpus striatum
(c) substantia nigra.

The basal ganglia is mainly concerned with muscular control.

The midbrain

The midbrain plays an important role in consciousness, attention and perception. It is the part of the brain which controls our habituation to common stimuli and alerts us to attend to novel stimuli. It thus prevents sensory overload. This mechanism is known as the reticular activating system. This means that it controls the activation of neural networks in response to appropriate stimuli.

The hindbrain

The hindbrain is, as the term suggests, situated behind the cerebrum. It is comprised of three sub-structures:

▶ *Cerebellum* – The cerebellum's role is skeleto-muscular control. Like the cerebrum, there are two separate hemispheres. The left cerebellum controls the right side of the body and the right cerebellum controls the left. It is also concerned with procedural memory functioning, i.e. storage and control of automatic skeleto-muscular movements.

▶ *Pons* – The term pons means bridge. This is the function which this part of the brain plays. It connects the two units of the cerebellum and so plays a role in co-ordination of the two sides of the body. It also connects the midbrain to the medulla oblongata

▶ *Medulla oblongata* – In this sub-structure the spinal nerves cross over, so that the left side of the body is connected to the right hemisphere and vice versa. It is this part of the brain that is responsible for reflex action. It also has an important part to play in respiratory control, cardiac functioning and facial movement, including smiling, chewing, coughing, swallowing and vomiting.

The spinal cord

The spinal cord is made up of 31 pairs of nerves. These nerves connect the body's peripheral nervous system with the brain (the **central nervous system**). The peripheral nervous system is made up of the:

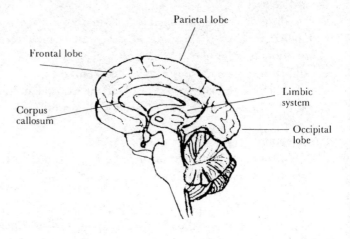

Figure 5. The brain from the side showing the limbic system.

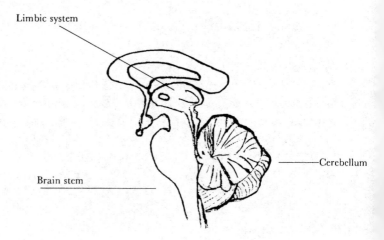

Figure 6. The brain stem, limbic system and cerebellum.

▶ somatic nervous system (SNS)

▶ autonomic nervous system (ANS).

The former sends messages to the skeleto-muscular system, for voluntary movement. The latter prepares the body's internal organs for action or rest.

The autonomic nervous system

There are two branches of the autonomic nervous system:

▶ *sympathetic branch* – sends signals to various parts of the body to prepare it for action against a threat

▶ *parasympathetic branch* – tells the same parts of the body that the threat is over.

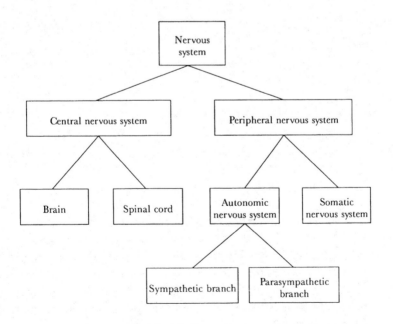

Figure 7. Diagram of the nervous system.

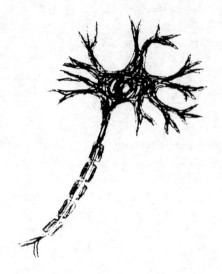

Figure 8. Diagram of a motor neuron.

Neurons

The brain and central nervous system are made up of neurons. Neurons consist of:

(a) cell body
(b) dendrites
(c) axon
(d) myelin sheath with nodes of ranvier (these are not present in all neurons)
(e) motor end plate (only relevant in motor neurons).

How do neurons communicate with each other?

With few exceptions, there is no direct contact between neurons. The gap between them is known as the synaptic cleft. The end of one neuron, known as the synaptic knob, contains small sacs, known as vesicles, which contain neurotransmitter substance. When the neuron is activated these are fired across the synaptic cleft and are received in similar vesicles by the receiving neuron. This is the way one neuron signals, and activates, another.

Tutorial

Practice questions

1. Name the four main parts of the brain.

2. Name the four different sections of the cerebrum.

3. What are the three principles by which the cortex functions?

4. What is the name of the fissure on each side of which lies the areas involved in control of motor behaviour?

5. Name at least six parts of the limbic system.

6. Name four functions which the thalamus serves.

Course work, revision and exam tips

When you have generated knowledge for each question, select out what you will use and what you will not. Evaluate the ideas in order of importance. Plan your essays. Begin writing and write solidly for the planned time for each essay. Readers can obtain additional tips for effective study from my book *Study and Learn*. Full details are given in the Further Reading section on page 168.

Bibliographical notes

[1] See Lashley 1929

15

Abnormal Psychology

One minute summary – Neuroses have anxiety as the central symptom. The most common affective disorders include mania, depression and manic depression. The most common diagnosed mental illness is schizophrenia. Various kinds of personality disorders have been identified. Mental retardation can have various causes. Behaviourists assume that maladaptive behaviour (symptoms) has been learned by conditioning, so that the cure (adaptive behaviour) must also be learned in the same way. Social learning theorists assume that mental illness is due to observing the maladapative behaviour rewarded in someone else's case. Psychoanalysts assume that mental disorders are due to psychic conflicts. Cognitive psychologists assume mental illness is due to faulty thinking. Social psychologists assume mental illness is due to social conditions. A psychobiological approach assumes biological causes and treats the illness in biological ways.

In this chapter you will learn about the:

▶ concept of mental illness
▶ syndromes
▶ behaviourist approach to treatment
▶ psychoanalytical approach to treatment
▶ cognitive approach to treatment
▶ social psychology approach to treatment
▶ humanist approach to treatment
▶ psychobiological approach to treatment.

Learning objectives

Once you have finished this chapter you should:

1. know what contributions to understanding abnormal psychology are made by each of the main schools of thought

2. be able successfully to tackle questions on abnormal psychology from different psychological perspectives

3. know the main theories and models of abnormal psychology.

The concept of mental illness

The concept of mental illness is controversial. Some argue that diagnosis is done to relieve the discomfort of others, rather than the patients themselves. People feel uncomfortable seeing highly unconventional behaviour.

Some societies even bring the expression of unsanctioned political views into this category and diagnose mental illness so as to intern the offenders.

Scrapping the term 'illness' doesn't help much. The term 'abnormality' provides its own problems. After all, some abnormalities are socially desirable – genius and creativity, for example.

Problems of diagnosis

Diagnosis is precariously unreliable, too. This is partly because there are only symptoms to go on. In physical medicine there are other indicators.

cognitive disorders	psychotic disorders	anxiety disorders
substance abuse	mood disorders	developmental disorders
somatoform disorders	dissociative disorders	impulse control disorders
adjustment problems	personality disorders	sleep disorders
sexual identity disorders	factitious disorders	
eating disorders	other unspecified disorders	

Table 2. Types of mental illness.

The two main sources of diagnostic criteria are these publications:

Diagnostic and Statistical Manual of Mental Disorders (DSM IV – R)
International Classification of Diseases (ICD – 10)

The syndromes

Each of the main kinds of psychological abnormality will now be identified and briefly described.

Neurotic anxiety

Neurotic anxiety is a general state of anxiousness which, unbeknown to the sufferer, is believed to be due to a fear of being overwhelmed by the **id.** The id is a psychoanalytical concept referring to an individual's animal instinct.

Moral anxiety

Moral anxiety is a similar state except that the cause is believed to be a fear of being overwhelmed by the **superego**. The superego is a psychoanalytical concept referring to the internalised parent.

Phobias

Phobias are conditions where certain objects produce unwarranted fear and avoidance behaviour. Anything can become a phobia object.

Phobia	*Fear object*
acrophobia	heights
agoraphobia	pain
astrophobia	thunder
arachnophobia	spiders
hydrophobia	water
photophobia	light
necrophobia	death
xenophobia	strangers
phobophobia	fear of fear itself
claustrophobia	small spaces
agraphobia	open spaces

Affective disorders

Affective disorders are mood disorders. There are three main kinds:

    mania   depression   manic depression

Mania
Manics display extreme euphoria, energy and excitement. They sleep little, they have rushes of unconnected and often grandiose ideas and are prone to things like spending sprees. They have abnormally low levels of inhibition and this may show in their sexual behaviour.

Depression
Depression is the opposite side of the coin to mania. It is not mere unhappiness; it is quite different. Indeed, depression involves a kind of emotional disengagement which, in a way, prevents the worst extremes of emotional pain being felt. Depression is associated with:

mental and physical sluggishness	lack of sex drive
negative thoughts	suicidal thoughts
lack of enthusiasm	lack of energy
lack of interest in life	poor sleep
loss of appetite	feelings of guilt

Seasonal affective disorder – SAD
Quite recently, a form of depression has been identified which appears to be associated with levels of light. Sufferers become progressively depressed as the time of year rolls on towards the longest day (midwinter) and progressively less depressed as it moves on from there towards the shortest day (midsummer).

Manic depression
Manic depression is a state wherein the sufferer alternates between mania and depression. At a chemical level their brains feature a low level of dopamine, noradrenaline and serotonin in times of depression and high levels in times of mania.

Obsessive compulsive disorder
Obsessions are uncontrollable intrusions of irrational thoughts. Compulsions are uncontrollable urges to do things. The two tend to be related.

Psychosomatic disorders
Psychosomatic disorders have both psychological and physical symptoms. Examples are ulcers, asthma and headaches.

Somatoform disorders

Somatoform disorders are mental disorders which have apparent physical symptoms; they are not real ones. Examples are:

paralysis	phantom pregnancy
speech problems	headaches
numbness	

Symptoms:

▶ are inconsistent
▶ only occur in particular people's presence
▶ do not seem to concern the sufferer.

Brief reactive psychoses

Brief reactive psychoses are illnesses which have psychosis type symptoms, but which are caused by stress and last for less than a month. Such conditions are examples of functional psychoses as opposed to what is known as organic psychoses.

Schizotypal disorders

Schizotypal disorders feature some of the symptoms usually associated with schizophrenia, but not the core ones.

Schizophreniform disorders

These have symptoms similar to schizophrenia, but are temporary, lasting less than six months.

Schizophrenia

Almost half of all diagnosed mental illness is schizophrenia. The term refers to a split from the self. It should not be confused with multiple personality. Theories about its causes include:

▶ genetics
▶ biochemical imbalance
▶ upbringing

Schizophrenia is generally incurable. Two-thirds of those who appear to recover tend to relapse.

Some authorities see it not as an illness, but a form of adaptation to conditions of life, which society curtails by means of drugs, for the sake of people who find schizophrenic behaviour disturbing.[2,3]

How is schizophrenia diagnosed?
One or more first rank symptoms[4] will usually result in a diagnosis of schizophrenia. They are, in order of importance:

1. passivity experiences
2. thought disturbances
3. primary delusions
4. hallucinations.

Other symptoms
► thought process disorder (side tracking on words in a conversation, neologisms and inappropriate interpretations)
► mood disturbances
► psychomotor disorders, including catalepsy and catatonic stupor
► lack of volition (low level of willpower, feeling and enthusiasm for life).[5]

Types of schizophrenia
Various types of schizoprhenia have been distinguished. They are:

► simple schizophrenia
► paranoid schizophrenia
► hebephrenic schizophrenia
► catatonic schizophrenia.

Simple schizophrenia
Simple schizophrenia is the commonest of all. It begins in adolescence and is characterised by a lack of volition, apathy, deterioration in academic and occupational performance and also social life. Many schizophrenics of this type become vagrants and, thus, may simply be seen as reclusive and eccentric.

Paranoid schizophrenia
Paranoid schizophrenia is characterised by delusions. They may be of persecution, or grandeur, or both.

Hebephrenic schizophrenia
Hebephrenic schizophrenia is the most bizarre of all the schizo-phrenia syndromes. Many of the schizophrenia diagnostic criteria tend to be present. Sufferers can be violent, but not necessarily so.

Catatonic schizophrenia
Catatonic schizophrenia is characterised by extremes in motor behaviour. It may be highly mobile, highly immobile, or alternating between the two.

Persistent delusional disorders (paranoia)
Persistent delusional disorder is where the only symptom is delusions.

Dissociative disorders
A dissociative personality is a split of personality. Two kinds can be dealt with here: dissociative identity disorder and dissociative fugue.

Dissociative identity disorder
Here the individual has more than one self. They may have a 'host self' and any number of subordinate selves. They tend not to be consciously aware of each other, although the subordinate selves contain a repressed version of the host self. They may change places frequently and quite suddenly on the appearance of stimuli which serve as cues.[6]

Dissociative fugue
Dissociative fugue is a condition whereby the sufferer tends to lose their memory. Sometimes they go away and start a new life, forming a new identity.

Personality disorders
Personality disorders are part of the personality. They have developed together. They cannot be remedied without changing the person. Three types will be dealt with here: paranoid personality, schizoid personality and psychopathy.

Paranoid personality
Paranoid people are:

overly suspicious of others   argumentative
hypersensitive   stubborn
easily humiliated and offended   self-important
prone to feelings of shame   self-sufficient
difficult to get on with   secretive
unreasonable   devious
prickly

They have high self-esteem, don't make friends easily and avoid involvement in groups.

Schizoid personality
The schizoid personality tends to have the following characteristics:

lack of affection   prone to fantasy
detachment   self-sufficient
incapable of intimate friendships   solitary
intellectual   unemotional
impractical

The schizoid personality is not to be confused with schizophrenia. It is common and there is no reason to assume that those whom it describes will ever become schizophrenic.

Psychopathy
The psychopath (sometimes referred to as affectionless psychopath or sociopath) tends to have the following personality characteristics:

amorality   poor social relations
excitement seeking   high level of social skill
impulsiveness   IQ above average
insensitivity   criminal tendencies
loveless sex   callousness
low frustration tolerance   poor job persistance
tendency to matrimonial violence

Mental retardation
Another category of psychological abnormality is mental retardation. Four types will be dealt with here: chronic brain damage, brain infections, degeneration of neural system and retardation.

Chronic brain damage
Damage can occur to any part of the brain as a result of accident, stroke, haemorrhage, or brain surgery. It can include:

memory impairment　　　　attentional disorders
intellectual impairment　　personality change
emotional instability.

Brain infections
A variety of infections can affect the brain. They range from relatively non-serious and temporary fevers to the highly damaging effects of bovine spongiform encephalopathy (BSE), untreated syphilis, meningitis and the brain version of herpes simplex, which can destroy the hippocampus with serious effects for memory.

Degeneration of the nervous system
Degeneration of the nervous system is caused by various diseases. They include:

Alzheimer's disease　　　　Parkinson's disease
Pick's disease　　　　　　　Huntington's chorea
　(similar to Alzheimer's)　Senile dementia.

Retardation
Retardation refers to faults in the brain due to abnormal development. Levels are categorised from mild to profound. Figure 9 shows the details.

Causes and cures
All the major schools of thought have their own views on the causes and cures (or controls and reliefs in some cases) of the various kinds of psychological maladies which have been identified.

Taking a behaviourist approach

Behaviourists believe that maladaptive behaviours become established because they have been in some way rewarded. Change this by making a more appropriate behaviour more rewarding, or less

Category	IQ	Abilities	% of total retardation sufferers
Mild	50-70	Language skill fairly normal. Need minimum help in day to day living. Capable of simple work.	80
Moderate	35-49	Language skills adequate. Need help/supervision in day to day life.	12
Severe	20-34	Language skills minimal. Need considerable help/supervision in everyday living. Condition becomes evident in early childhood as slow development.	7
Profound	20 or less	Little, or no language ability. Require constant, comprehensive care.	1

Figure 9. Levels of retardation.

punishing, and you remove the illness. Two of the main behaviourist treatments are:

1. behaviour modification
2. behaviour therapy

Behaviour modification
This refers to a highly rigid and structured approach in which there are eight steps:

1. statement of maladaptive behaviour
2. statement of behavioural goal
3. measure maladaptive behaviour under untreated conditions
4. decision on method
5. plan of treatment
6. commencement of treatment
7. progress monitoring
8. progress evaluation and treatment where necessary.

Behaviour therapy
Behaviour therapy refers to a number of individual techniques for specific problems.

The behaviourist approach to phobias

Behaviourists assume phobias arise from accidental associations. These occur when we have a traumatic emotional experience and our subconscious mind simultaneously picks up an unconnected object in our peripheral vision.

▶ *Example* – Suppose, as a child, something frightened you. Perhaps your parents were shouting at each other, or perhaps you suddenly lost sight of your mother and thought you were lost. You would not have been aware of what your peripheral vision was picking up. There might have been a spider, a beetle, or some other harmless object. Whenever in the future such an object would appear its associated feeling would be relived – *fear*.

The remedy is to replace the association between the phobic object and fear with an association with a feeling of calm. There are three types of technique for this:

▶ systematic desensitisation
▶ implosion
▶ flooding.

Systematic desensitisation

A negative emotion can be neutralised by inducing a positive emotion. The individual is exposed to progressively increasing doses of the phobic object while the negative reactions are more than compensated for by the inducement of positive feelings. An arachnophobic might first be exposed to a cartoon picture of a spider and the small amount of negative reaction more than compensated for by a warm environment, comforting music, and words of reassurance.

Later, a slightly higher level of exposure would be applied, a picture of a real spider, for example. This will be followed by exposure to a real money-spider and so on.

Implosion

Rather than progressively increasing exposure, the patient is encouraged to imagine the presence of the phobic object – and imagine it even worse than it is. The technique assumes there is an absolute ceiling to anxiety level and that, being fuelled by energy, it must run short of fuel and decline. The declining fear with which the object is associated will gradually extinguish the phobia.

Flooding

Flooding is the same as implosion except that, instead of imagination, the real thing is used. An arachnophobic individual, for example, would be exposed to the biggest spider that could be found.

All these methods can be augmented by the use of hypnotism.

Stimulus association

Sometimes individuals need to overcome compulsions to perform certain behaviours. Behaviour will be habitually performed if it has become associated with a reward, i.e. a pleasurable feeling. When such behaviour is inappropriate, by inducing an individual to perform it when the incentive value is close to zero, or even below it, that particular behaviour will become associated with little or no reward.

Aversion therapy

A more powerful method of removing a compulsion to perform undesirable behaviours is known as aversion therapy. This amounts to deliberately inducing an association between an undesirable behaviour and a negative feeling. It is used for treating conditions like alcoholism and sexual perversions. If alcoholics are prescribed a drug that will make them nauseous if they drink alcohol then an association will be registered in the brain between alcohol and severely negative feeling.[7]

Covert sensitisation

It is the subconscious mind which records these associations and it will record them just the same whether they are real or imaginary. Covert sensitisation requires the individual to imagine a negative consequence rather than inducing a negative consequence by drugs, or other means.

Shaping behaviour

Sometimes the objective is not so much to eliminate or replace behaviour forms, but, rather, to gradually change them in a particular direction. Behaviour therapy is a method which can be used. It involves rewarding behaviour which appears to be shaping up in the right direction just as a parent does to a child, teaching it gradually to develop into a responsible adult.

Token economy programmes

Hospitals that deal with behavioural problems of various natures sometimes use token economy programs.[8] Patients are rewarded when they show evidence of desired behaviour. Anorexia nervosa patients, for example, may be rewarded on meeting set targets of weight increase.

Taking a psychoanalytical approach

The psychoanalytical school of thought sees all neurotic illnesses as being caused by psychic conflicts between the *id* and the *superego*. The symptoms are the results of attempts to cope with these. Some of the ways the psyche deals with these are by projection, displacement and repression.

Projection

This term refers to a neurotic tendency to deal with feelings, or qualities you feel you should not have, by inferring them as being present in someone, or something else instead. Phobics are an example of this. The behaviourist view is that virtually anything can become a phobic object, but in psychoanalytical theory the neurotic mind carefully selects its phobic objects on the basis of symbolism.

Displacement

Displacement is a neurotic way of dealing with a psychic conflict by imagining a more tangible problem.

Repression

Repression refers to burying a psychic conflict in the unconscious mind, so that you are unaware that it is there. The trouble is, it festers beneath the surface and can produce any one or more of a variety of symptoms. These range from the more psychological ones, such as anxiety, to highly physical ones, such as psoriasis.

It is repression which lies at the root of neurotic illness. Freud believed the psychic conflicts concerned were of a sexual and possibly aggressive nature and buried in the unconscious during childhood.

Psychoanalytical cures for neurosis

Psychoanalysts believe neuroses are consequences of failure to adapt appropriately to psychic conflicts. The patient represses them, rather than facing them and coming to terms with them. The cure lies in bringing them into conscious awareness and helping the individual deal appropriately with them.

Dream analysis

Freud believed that dreams are a way of expressing the id's desires and fears which have been frustrated, or hidden from consciousness in waking life. Likewise, it is a way of expressing fears and conflicts that the conscious mind has buried in order to hide from them. By a structured analysis of dreams Freud believed that significant conflicts can be pinpointed. Freud believed the structure of dreams consists of: symbolism, displacement, and condensation.

- ▶ *Symbolism* – Psychoanalysts believe that the mind has an inherent symbolism. It carefully selects certain objects to represent aspects of its conflicts. These symbols appear in dreams and help the psychoanalyst locate where the conflict lies.

- ▶ *Displacement* – This has already been referred to in respect of behaviour in the neurotic's waking life. It is basically the same in dreams. Feelings which an individual feels severely uncomfortable about are, instead, mapped onto someone else in dreams, often a close friend or relative.

- ▶ *Condensation* – This refers to the fabric of dreams. Dreamscapes (environments of dreams) tend to have a strangeness about them, familiar yet unfamiliar at the same time. This is because they contain all of the situational junk that the mind has encountered during the day before the dream. The function of the fabric of the dream is merely to provide a context in which the meaningful stuff can happen.

It is the symbols and displacements that provide clues to conflicts underlying neurotic illness.

Free association

Free association is a technique in which an individual is encouraged to say the first things that come into their head, without any rational attempt to recall particular things or any attempt to order them. When sudden blocks occur in the flow of data, psychoanalysts infer that they are connected with important psychic conflicts. They probe around these points to try to uncover evidence of the problem.

Transference

Once the repressed conflict has been revealed and located in the childhood of their client, a psychoanalyst will encourage them to relive that part of their childhood, complete with the conflict concerned. This time, however, they will be helped to deal with it consciously and come to terms with it. It may be reasonably well established that the conflict arose out of a particular interpersonal relationship. Where this is so, the patient is encouraged to treat the psychoanalyst as the other party concerned.

Brief focal therapy

This is based on the essential principles of psychoanalysis. The main difference is that it is less intensive and less formal.

Group therapy

Group therapy is based on psychoanalytical principles. Group members are encouraged to explore the conflicts in their psyches and transfer the object of them onto another member of the group. That person has to play the role of the person with whom the conflict took place, e.g. parent. In this way, they relive the conflicts and deal with them in more adaptive ways than they had previously.

Fundamental to this method of treating maladaptive behaviour is the recognition of three parts of the psyche:

child	adult	parent

Individuals learn which part of the psyche is responsible for behaviours they wish to change. They are taught to displace that part from the executive slot of their consciousness by responding in a purely rational, rather than emotive, or conditioned way.

Taking a cognitive approach

The cognitive approach to therapy focuses on the potential for curing psychological disorders by directly teaching the individuals concerned to think in more appropriate ways. Six different cognitive therapies will be outlined here:

1. rational emotive therapy
2. personal construct therapy
3. thought stopping technique
4. automatic thoughts, treatment of
5. cognitive restructuring
6. self instructional training.

Rational Emotive Therapy (RET)
Rational emotive therapy seeks to replace irrational thinking with rational thinking. It involves hunting down irrational self-beliefs, for example that making mistakes, or failing to live up to certain standards, renders a person worthless. Individuals are encouraged to think positive things about themselves and to write them down to 'concrete' them.[9]

Personal construct therapy
According to personal construct theory, we have to make estimates of the way things are and the consequences of taking different actions. These stored interpretations amount to a series of personal constructs. We continuously try to improve our knowledge so that we can predict more accurately.

▶ *Personal construct system too loose* – Problems arise when we fail to update our personal construct system to take account of what we should have learned. A psychological disorder may be defined as a personal construct system that persists, unadapted, in spite of evidence invalidating it.

▶ *Personal construct system too tight* – As we learn more about the world we tighten our personal constructs, to take account of the greater accuracy with which we may expect to make predictions. Sometimes we go too far. We assume that because particular consequences followed particular actions in the past this will always be the case.

Personal construct therapists investigate, with their clients, the appropriateness of their personal construct systems and help them to tighten, or loosen them where appropriate.

Methods used by personal construct therapists
The personal construct therapist is usually prepared to use a wide range of methods, but principally:

▶ self characterisation
▶ fixed role sketch
▶ fixed role enactment.

The client is encouraged to write a self-characterisation. The therapist writes a counter version of it. They then work together to arrive at a form of characterisation somewhere between the two which the client can accept as liveable ('fixed role sketch'). The client is then encouraged to live that character for a set time ('fixed role enactment'). At the end of it success and relief of symptoms is measured.

The repertory grid
Kelly devised a table known as a *repertory grid* for assessing a person's personal construct system. Using a specific formula, the client plots the main attributes of people who make up their perceived social world. The results are factor analysed to remove duplications. At the end of a course of therapy, a new table is constructed and compared with the old one.

Thought stopping technique

Where irrational thoughts trouble an individual, Wolpe[10] suggests that they should be encouraged to let the irrational thinking take place while the therapist bides their time ready to shout STOP! The client is encouraged to repeat the command. Gradually the audible repeated command by the client is replaced by a silent command.

Cognitive restructuring

Cognitive psychologists assume that depression arises from inappropriate thinking about the relationship between three things, the so-called 'cognitive triad of depression':

1. the self
2. the world
3. the future.

Depressed people tend to hold negative beliefs about each of these. Cognitive therapists encourage them to test these beliefs against empirical data and rational argument with a view to seeing them more realistically.

Self instructional training

The assumption on which this therapy is based is that all thought is silent speech. The steps in the therapy are:

► help the client to see the faulty mental statements, or instructions that underlie their problem

► help them write new ones

► help them to practise acting out their revised instructional behaviour

► encourage them to give themselves mental warnings against reversion to the original, inappropriate instructions

► encourage them to act out the new instructions in a real life situation

► debrief and evaluate.

Helping clients practise acting out replacement instructions involves three stages:

1. audible verbal instructions
2. silently mouthed instructions
3. completely covert instructions (mentally, without sound or lip movements).[11]

Taking a social psychological approach

Social conditions play a major role in psychological disorders. We live in a social world and it is to this we have to adapt. Psychological disorders are maladaptations to social conditions.

Psychodrama

This is a technique developed by J. L. Moreno. Unresolved conflicts between an individual and others may be repressed and result in anxiety. Psychodrama provides opportunities and guidance to work through these conflicts and adapt appropriately.

A typical psychodrama therapy session contains the following elements:

- the plot
- role allocation
- doubling
- mirroring
- interrogation.

The plot will contain a conflict important to a member present. Some members perform the roles of those people with whom the unresolved conflict exists and others help to amplify their behaviour. The drama leader provides guidance on what the protagonist's reactions and feelings ought to be. After the drama, the protagonist is encouraged to explore their reactions and feelings.

Social learning theory

The behaviourist assumption of reward and punishment as the main determinants of behaviour underlies social learning theory. The focus, however, is on what we witness in the cases of other people. If we see another person benefiting from a particular behaviour we are likely to copy it. If we see them being punished we will be unlikely to copy it.

How social learning theory explains phobias, for example, is that phobic people witness someone exhibiting a severe fear of spiders, or some other phobia object, and receiving sympathy and support because of it. They imitate such behaviour, in anticipation of the same kinds of reward.

A phobic person can be coaxed to overcome their fear and touch a phobia object if they see someone else do it.[12]

Taking a humanist approach

If we act in a way inconsistent with our self beliefs we suffer anxiety as a result. Alternatively, we may deny the reality and change our conception of the way things are to make them consistent with our behaviour. Our self-concept then becomes out of touch with reality. This, in itself, leads to defensive behaviour.

If inconsistency is minimal it can result in neurosis. If it is considerable the consequences can amount to psychotic disorder involving disintegration of the personality.

Client centred therapy (CCT)
Client centred therapy derives from the work of Carl Rogers.[13] The underlying assumption is that psychological disorder is due to the self-concept and the ideal self becoming out of synch. When this happens the result is low self-esteem.

Everybody needs the approval of certain others around them. Sometimes, however, it is only given on condition that the individual behaves in a certain way. This may be inconsistent with their true self.

Client centred therapy involves facilitating conditions in which the individual can obtain the experience of unconditional positive regard while expressing behaviour, attitudes and beliefs which are true to them.

Encounter groups

The parts of the psyche can be out of synch, because an individual has built defensive responses which prevent them from acting in a way which is true to their ideal self. It may be that they are no longer appropriate responses, or in fact, that they never have been.

Encounter groups enable such individuals to practise behaving without such barriers in place in safe conditions, before applying it to real social situations. They will then know what responses to expect when they do so for real.

Taking a psychobiological approach

Psychobiological approaches to curing psychological disorder include:

▶ chemotherapy
▶ electro convulsive treatment (ECT)
▶ psychosurgery.

Chemotherapy

There is always a neurochemical aspect to psychological disorders. Sometimes this is the root cause of the problem. At others times it is a consequence of a reaction to conditions of life. By correcting this imbalance at least the symptoms may be suppressed, and in some cases the original cause controlled.

The drugs used for treating psychological disorders work in different ways:

(a) activating neurotransmitter chemicals
(b) prevent their re-uptake, so as to prolong their effect
(c) blocking their effect.

Treating anxiety

The main drugs which tend to be used to control anxiety are diazepam and chlordiazepoxide. These act on the limbic system and brain stem. This kind of drug should only be used where anxiety is the essence of the illness.

Treating depression

There are a number of drug types for treating depression, depending on the form of the illness concerned, i.e. clinical, endogenous, or manic.

Drug	How it works
Tricyclic	Blocks the re-uptake of relevant neurotransmitters
Monoamine oxidase inhibitors	Blocks the effect of monoamine oxidase enzyme
Lithium carbonate	The process is not fully understood, but it stabilises neural activity in manic depressives

Figure 10. Drugs for treating depression.

Treating schizophrenia

Schizophrenia is treated with major tranquillisers, such as chlorpromazine. The drug accumulates in the brain stem and is released gradually. There are significant side effects, especially longer term. The most noticeable is, perhaps, uncontrollable motor activity, including hand shake and involuntary mouth movement.

Electro convulsive therapy (ECT)

ECT involves applying an electric shock to the brain. It can take two forms:

▶ unilateral treatment involves one hemisphere only
▶ bilateral involves both hemispheres.

It was originally developed as a treatment for epilepsy and schizophrenia. It did not prove very successful in treating these conditions, but it has proved quite successful in treating endogenous depression. Nobody fully understands why. There are three possibilities:

1. It causes chemical change in the brain.

2. It causes memory loss and this necessitates mental restructuring

by the patient, to compensate. The restructuring may be more adaptive than the original structuring.

3. It is a process of *conditioning* – punishing maladaptive behaviour.[14]

Ethical considerations
It has been argued that electro convulsive therapy should not be used because it is not fully understood how it works. Perhaps the main disadvantage is the memory loss caused by this treatment (retrograde amnesia). On the other hand, it improves quality of life for depressives. It is quick, easy and relatively cheap to carry out and beneficial effects are seen straight away.

Psychosurgery

Psychosurgery involves cutting or destroying brain tissue in selected regions. It is generally accepted that this should be used in only the most extreme cases of psychological disorder, where the level of distress is very high and all other methods have failed. There are various forms of the operation:

▶ amygdalotomy
▶ prefrontal lobotomy
▶ stereotactic limbic leucotomy
▶ stereotactic tractotomy
▶ transorbital leucotomy.

The prefrontal lobotomy was the first form of this operation used. It involved making a hole in the skull and, through this, penetrating the frontal lobe of the brain to destroy selected areas of brain tissue.

Later, the transorbital leucotomy, was developed. Here, entry to the brain is made through the eye sockets.

More recent developments have involved greater precision in the location and amount of brain tissue for destruction. The operations tend to concentrate on various parts of the limbic system and have become known as stereotactic, limbic leucotomies.

The stereotactic tractotomy uses a radioactive substance to destroy brain tissue, rather than a neural lance.

Ethical considerations
There are important ethical concerns about this form of treatment.
Here are some of the main issues:

(a) irreversibility
(b) considerable side effects
(c) whose benefit is it being carried out for?
(d) often used on those who cannot give informed consent
(e) potential for abuse of civil liberties.

Some neurosurgeons have expressed a willingness to use the
technique as a means of controlling violent crime.[15] This issue
was dramatised in the Jack Nicholson film, *One Flew Over The
Cuckoo's Nest*.

Tutorial

Practice questions

1. List ten kinds of phobia.

2. List three kinds of affective disorder.

3. How is schizophrenia diagnosed? State four principal criteria.

4. List three types of personality disorder.

5. List three types of cognitive therapy.

6. Name three psychobiological approaches to treating mental
    disorders.

Seminar discussion
How useful is the concept of mental illness?

Practical assignment
Find a newspaper story about someone with an eating disorder,
alcoholism, depression, or personality disorder. Evaluate what is

written in the article in the light of what you have learnt about psychological disorders. Consider what kinds of therapy would be appropriate to treat this condition and why.

Course work, revision and exam tips

Don't leave the exam room early. Exams are set so that they challenge even the brightest and most well prepared students. There are always useful ways you can use any time you have left.

After the exam, do a quick assessment of how well you did and any adjustments you need to make to your revision and exam strategies. Then forget about the exam, don't extend the post mortem any further. You will only dwell on what you didn't manage to do. This will simply increase your anxiety level and condition you against exams by associating them with anxiety.

Bibliographical notes

[1]   Spitzer et al. 1978
[2]   Szasz 1962
[3]   Laing 1967
[4]   Schneider 1959
[5]   Slater et al. 1969
[6]   Thigpen and Cleckley 1954
[7]   Kleinmuntz 1980
[8]   Ayllon and Azrin 1968

[9]   Ellis 1973
[10]   Wolpe 1978
[11]   Meichenbaum 1973
[12]   Bandura 1969
[13]   Rogers 1973
[14]   Benton 1981
[15]   Taylor 1992

Glossary

Acrophobia Fear of heights.

Activity theory A prescriptive theory that old people should seek to maintain their role count. Old age takes away some social roles, but it provides opportunities for others.

Adolescence A stage of development falling between the age ranges of roughly 12 and 25.

Affective disorders Abnormalities of mood.

Agoraphobia Fear of pain.

Astrophobia Fear of thunder.

Aversion therapy Deliberately inducing an association between an undesirable behaviour and a negative feeling. It is used for treating conditions like alcoholism and sexual perversions.

Behaviourism A psychological perspective from which it is assumed that all mental behaviour can be explained in terms of *reward and punishment*. If a particular behavioural form is rewarded it is likely to be repeated.

Claustrophobia Fear of small spaces.

Cocktail party effect When a person becomes aware of their name being spoken, or their personal details being talked about in conversation they have not otherwise been attending to.

Cognitive disorders Psychological disorders due to maladaptive thinking.

Cognitive dissonance A drive to reduce a discrepancy between thought and behaviour.

Confabulation When individuals are in a state of extreme emotional arousal they tend to make up information which will make their account of events coherent, consistent and logical. This is not exactly culpable lying, for, at the time, they may not be very aware of the falsity of their statements.

Conscience A personal source of inhibition and guilt.

Dècalage The staggered pattern in which children develop conservation abilities.

Declarative memory The general knowledge store.

Dementia A syndrome involving severe memory loss, states of confusion and frustration. It affects mainly the elderly, but occasionally occurs earlier in life.

Depression A kind of emotional disengagement associated with mental and physical sluggishness and negative thoughts.

Developmental disorder A mental disorder which has its roots in the process of psychological development.

Drive An internal motive force underlying behaviour.

Ego The intelligent part of the consciousness, the part that manages the conflicting forces of desire and restraint.

Emotion Emotions are responses to events. While the mind alone can provide us with an understanding of things, emotions give us a physical feeling about them, so that we may wish to repeat the experiences, or avoid them.

Episodic memory The mental store which appears to hold autobiographical data, including time, place and experience.

Feature detectors Brain cells which detect points, straight lines and curves.

Fixation When part of the psyche fails to move from one stage of psychological development to the next, contrary to normal development.

Glucoreceptors Devices which detect the level of glucose in the bloodstream.

Habituation When repeated amounts of a stimulus reduce the level of sensitivity to it.

Homeostasis A drive to maintain a constant supply of energy and fluid in the body.

Humanism The psychological perspective from which it is assumed that all mental behaviour, normal and abnormal, can be explained by people's drive to actualise their potential.

Hydrophobia The fear of water.

Hypothalamus A tiny part of the brain which is involved in the control of heat, hunger, water balance, agression and pleasure.

Hypothesis A postulated connection between two or more variables for the purpose of testing. Psychologists formulate at least two hypotheses each time they wish to test an association between two variables. These are known as the target hypothesis (H_1) and the null hypothesis (H_2). The first says the data will show evidence that a suspected association exists, the second says it will not. It is the latter hypothesis which is tested.

Intelligence A general cognitive ability, variously defined, but tending to refer to an individual's relative ability to learn, reason and adapt to, and exploit, their environment.

Intelligence quotient (IQ) A measure of relative intelligence level. It is named thus because, in its original form, it was the quotient of *mental age multiplied by 100 and divided by chronological age*. However, despite the fact that they are still referred to as IQ scores, modern intelligence test scores are based on deviation from the mean.

Limbic system A number of brain structures lying below the corpus callosum. They include the hypothalamus, mamillary bodies, cingulate gyrus, hippocampus, amygdala, fornix and olfactory bulb.

Lobotomy An operation to destroy brain tissue, in the treatment of mental illness.

Long-term potentiation. The physiological process believed to underlie storage in long-term memory. It involves high frequency stimulation of the pre-synaptic mechanism, which causes neurons to release glutamate. For LTP to occur, exactly the right amount of ions have to be present in the receptor vesicles. A substance known as NMDA is thought to be involved in bringing this about.

Maladaption Failure to adapt normally, or appropriately, to conditions of life.

Mania A mental disorder characterised by extreme euphoria, energy and excitement.

Manic depression A state wherein the sufferer alternates between mania and depression.

Negative reinforcement Conditioning by opportunities to avoid pain.

Neogenesis The principal component in intelligence revealed by factor analysis of the concept's dimensions.

Norm The commonest level at which, or manner in which, any particular behaviour (physical, or mental) tends to be performed in particular types of situation, in particular cultures. Norms are used as yardsticks to judge normality of behaviours.

Parallel processing Carrying out more than one function at a time.

Phobophobia Fear of fear.

Procedural memory Storage and control of automatic skeleto-muscular movements.

Projection A neurotic tendency to deal with feelings, or qualities which an individual feels they should not have by inferring them as being present in someone, or something else instead.

Psychoanalysis The psychological perspective from which it is assumed that all mental behaviour is explainable in terms of attempts to protect the ego.

Psychobiology The psychological perspective from which it is assumed that all mental behaviour is explainable in terms of biological factors.

Psychopath A personality type characterised by: callousness, amorality, impulsiveness, insensitivity, low frustration tolerance, violence, and criminal tendencies.

Psychosomatic disorders Disorders which, though they have their roots in psychological problems, have both psychological and physical symptoms.

Repression Burying a psychic conflict in the unconscious mind, so that you are not even consciously aware that it is there.

Schemata (**singular** *schema*) Schemata are configurations of permanently modified neural pathways as a result of experience. They are mappings of experience into the neural system of the brain. As a result of them an individual can relive, or recall, an experience after it has happened.

Schizophrenia A major, and usually incurable, mental disorder involving a split from the self. The main syptoms include passivity experiences, thought disturbance, delusions and hallucinations.

Self actualisation Harmonising discrepant micro-level selves, bringing the actual self-concept more into line with the ideal self-concept, for example. This can involve striving to achieve more, or it can mean lowering one's expectations.

Semantic memory The memory store which contains such things as: concepts, facts, language, rules and words.

Serial processing Carrying out one function at a time.

Social exchange theory A prescriptive theory which suggests that the conditions of old age should be seen in terms of the roles which made an individual an economically active member of society being relinquished in exchange for freedom from responsibility and increased leisure time.

Social psychology The psychological perspective from which it is assumed that all mental behaviour, normal or abnormal, can be explained by reference to social conditions.

Synesthesia The crossing of senses. Some people see particular colours when they hear particular sounds, for example.

Thalamus The thalamus refers to two grey, egg-shaped bodies in the brain. They are involved in regulation of consciousness and in relaying information from the ears, eyes and body to the cortex.

Theoretical construct A statement supported by evidence that two concepts are related in some way.

Theory Two or more interrelated theoretical constructs. Theories explain phenomona in a proportion of cases. If they explained all incidences they would be laws rather than theories.

Web Sites for Students

Note – Neither the author nor the publisher is responsible for content or opinions expressed on linked remote sites. The following notes are simply intended to offer some starting points for students exploring psychology on the internet. Also, please remember that the internet is a fast-evolving environment, and links may come and go. If you have some favourite sites you would like to see mentioned in future editions of this book, please write to us (address on back cover). Happy surfing!

Academic Psychology Departments in Britain and Ireland
http://www.psych.bangor.ac.uk/deptpsych/BIPsychDepts/BIP-sychDepts.html
This useful site offers pointers to departments of psychology in the British Isles.

Addiction Research
http://www.gbhap-us.com/Addiction_Research/
Addiction Research is a Gordon and Breach cross-disciplinary journal which examines the effects of context on the use and misuse of substances, and on the nature of intoxications of all kinds.

American Psychological Association
http://www.apa.org/
The APA, based in Washington, DC, is the largest scientific and professional organisation for psychology in the United States and is the world's largest association of psychologists. Its membership includes more than 155,000 researchers, educators, clinicians, consultants, and students. Through its divisions in 50 subfields of psychology and affiliations with 59 state, territorial, and Canadian provincial associations, APA works to advance psychology as a science and profession, and as a means of promoting human welfare.

Association for Behavior Analysis

http://www.wmich.edu/aba/

This is an American organisation dedicated to promoting the experimental, theoretical, and applied analysis of behaviour. It encompasses contemporary scientific and social issues, theoretical advances, and the dissemination of professional and public information. It provides a forum for twenty-one special interest groups.

Behaviorists for Social Responsibility

http://www.bfsr.org

This is a Special Interest Group of the Association for Behaviour Analysis, dedicated to increasing applications of the science of behaviour and cultural analysis to social justice issues.

Birkbeck College Department of Psychology

http://www.psyc.bbk.ac.uk/general/resources.html

This page offers a useful collection of psychology resources for students. There are links to UK academic departments, conference pages, journals, societies and more.

Brain and Cognitive Sciences at the MIT

http://web-bcs.mit.edu/

This is a web site of the Massachusetts Institute of Science & Technology. It contains links to people, curriculum, research areas, research centres, resources, calendar, publications, and contact information.

British Association for Counselling

http://www.bac.co.uk/

The BAC, which is open to individuals and organisations, aims to promote counselling throughout society. It works to maintain and raise standards of training and practice, provide professional support, and publish directories and other information about counselling. Site links include contact details, index, membership, publications, register, accreditation, looking for a counsellor, job file, principles of counselling, advertising, divisions, training, and research network.

British Association for Sexual & Marital Therapy

http://www.basmt.org.uk/

BASMT aims to advance the education and training of persons engaged in sexual, marital and relationship therapy, to promote research in the fields of marriage and other intimate relationships, and to advance the education of the public about sexual, marital and relationship therapy. Its web site provides details of latest news objectives, constitution, definitions, code of ethics, European codes, complaint procedure, training courses, membership details, supervisor criteria, journal, bulletin, conferences, information sheets and list of therapists.

British Psychological Society

http://www.bps.org.uk/

The British Psychological Society was founded in 1901 and now has 32,000 members. This is a practical and detailed site which will take you quickly to almost every aspect of psychology, whether as a patient, a professional, a job applicant or a student - conferences, meetings, advertising, seminars, professional directories, divisions, sections, special groups and lots more. Look out for *Psychology Online*, the Society's new monthly electronic publication.

Cerebral Institute of Discovery

http://www.cerebral.org

This site offers a collection of neurological links, ranging from brain research studies and pharmocology to treatment options and technologies for those with neurological disturbances.

Clinical Neurophysiology on the Internet

http://www.neurophys.com/

The site offers a well presented and comprehensive range of international professional and academic links to all aspects of neurophysiology on the internet.

Cognitive & Psychological Usenet Newsgroups

http://matia.stanford.edu/cogsci/usenet.html

Don't forget to check out the newsgroups as a source of information and contacts. This excellent list of usenet links has been created within Stanford University, USA.

Cognitive Psychology: a Web Directory

http://server.bmod.athabascau.ca/html/aupr/cognitive.htm
Another excellent resource for students, albeit with a strong
American bias.

Cognitive Psychology Online Lab

http://www.psych.purdue.edu/~coglab/
This site contains modules including memory search task, mental
rotation task, receptive field tutorial, and memory span.

Cognitive Psychology at the University of Edinburgh

http://www.cogsci.ed.ac.uk/school
This is the web site of Edinburgh University's School of Cognitive
Science. It is concerned with the study of language and related
cognitive processes from a computational perspective.

Cognitive Psychology at the University of Exeter

http://www.ex.ac.uk/CogSci/
In 1991, the single honours degree in Cognitive Science was started
at the University of Exeter. Hosted by the (then) departments of
Psychology and Computer Science, Exeter became one of the first
British universities to offer a degree in this challenging and relatively
new field.

Cognitive Psychology at the University of Sussex

http://www.cogs.susx.ac.uk/index.html
The School of Cognitive and Computing Sciences at the University
of Sussex at Brighton is a centre for multi-disciplinary research and
teaching in artificial intelligence, computer science, linguistics,
philosophy and psychology. Undergraduate, masters and research
degrees are available in all the above subjects.

Cognitive Science Society

http://www.umich.edu/~cogsci/
This organisation brings together researchers from many fields who
share the goal of understanding the nature of the human mind.

Connexions

http://www.shef.ac.uk/~phil/connex/

This is an interactive site, electronic journal and discussion list for philosophers and cognitive scientists, based at the University of Sheffield.

Facts for Families

http://www.aacap.org/web/aacap/factsFam/

The site offers information about psychiatric disorders affecting children and adolescents. There are 46 explanatory sheets covering issues such as the depressed child, teen suicide, step-family problems and child sexual abuse.

Freud Web

http://www.stg.brown.edu/projects/hypertext/landow/HTat-Brown/freud/Freud_OV.html

Unfortunately this is a very long URL, but if you can manage it you will find links to all aspects of Freud's life and work. They include biography, chronology, cultural context, religion, philosophy, literary relations, theory of the mind, levels of consciousness, libido, id, ego, superego, defence mechanisms, psychosexual stages of development, and repression.

Freudian Links

http://www.mii.kurume-u.ac.jp/~leuers/Freud.htm

This is a really first class index of Freud and psychoanalysis-related resources on the internet. The information is international, comprehensive, well organised and well presented, and the functionally designed pages are quick to load. Well worth bookmarking.

FreudNet

http://www.interport.net/nypsan/

This is a library site for information about Freud, psychoanalysis and related topics.

Hypnosis in the UK

http://www.hypnosis.org.uk

This is quite a detailed site about hypnosis in the UK - history and development, benefits, therapists, training, seminars, books, links and more.

Institute of Neurology, London
http://www.ion.ucl.ac.uk/
This is a good source of information of neurology in theory and practice. The Institute is affiliated to University College, London.

International Journal of Psychoanalysis
http://www.ijpa.org/
This journal was founded in 1920 by Ernest Jones, under the direction of Sigmund Freud. It is a peer reviewed journal published six times a year since its merger with *The International Review of Psycho-Analysis* in 1994.

InterPsych
http://www.shef.ac.uk/uni/projects/gpp/index.html
InterPsych is a non-profit cyber-organisation first conceived at the University of Sheffield in December 1993. It aims to enable individuals to communicate and contribute to ideas in health, behaviour, cognition and education.

Jean Piaget Society
http://www.piaget.org/
Established in 1970, the Society has an international, interdisciplinary membership of scholars, teachers and researchers interested in exploring the developmental construction of human knowledge. It was named in honour of the Swiss developmentalist, Jean Piaget, who made major theoretical and empirical contributions to our understanding of the origins and evolution of knowledge.

Max Planck Institute for Psycholinguistics
http://www.mpi.nl
Based in the Netherlands, the Institute - one of about 70 across Europe - explores research in the study of mental processes involved in language production, comprehension, acquisition, and cognition.

Mental Health
http://www.mentalhealth.com/
The goal of this internet site is to improve understanding, diagnosis, and treatment of mental illness throughout the world. You can use this site to explore descriptions, symptoms, diagnosis and articles, and link to many related sites on the internet.

Methods in Behavioral Research
http://methods.fullerton.edu
This site contains a text for research methods courses in psychology and other behavioural sciences.

National Association of Cognitive-Behavioral Therapists
http://www.nacbt.org
The NACBT provides certification, seminars, and networking for cognitive-behavioural therapists. Student and professional memberships are available.

National Association of School Psychologists
http://www.naspweb.org/
This US organisation aims to promote educationally and psychologically healthy environments for all children and youth. It supports research-based, effective programmes designed to prevent problems, enhance independence, and promote optimal learning.

Neuro-Linguistic Programming
http://www.nlp.com/NLP/
Find out more about this young branch of psychology, most heavily resembling cognitive psychology. It overlaps with hypnosis and hypnotism.

Neurosciences on the Internet
http://ivory.lm.com/~nab/
This is an excellent, searchable and browsable index of neuroscience resources available on the internet. You will find hundreds of well organised links to neurobiology, neurology, neurosurgery, psychiatry, psychology, cognitive science sites and information on human neurological diseases.

Open University - Knowledge Media Institute
http://kmi.open.ac.uk/
KMI runs a broad programme of research into new learner-centred technologies, including internet-enhanced collaboration media, multimedia environments for disabled learners, intelligent agents, organisational memories, digital documents, scientific visualisation and simulation tools, informal and formal representations of knowledge - in short, innovative approaches to sharing, accessing, and understanding knowledge.

Psychnet
http://psychnet.unn.ac.uk
Psychnet is an embryonic network of university psychology departments based in the north east of England aimed at developing and promoting the competencies and skills of their graduates. Psychology instructors, mentors and professionals are encouraged to visit its academic staff page to review crucial resources and participate in an online discussion.

Psycholinguistics
http://www.yehouda.com/linguistics.html
This web site offers a spirited discussion of various aspects of psycholinguistics.

Psychological Tutorials Online
http://psych.hanover.edu/Krantz/tutor.html
This interesting page contains links to hypertext tutorials in psychology, covering every aspect of study and revision from Auditory Perception to Visual Demonstrations.

Psychology and Cognitive Sciences on the Internet
http://www.ke.shinshu-u.ac.jp/psych/index.html
This very useful Japanese-based site contains more than 1,400 URL links related to cognitive sciences and psychology. You can follow its hierarchies of headings, or do a keyword search. It is hard to tell exactly how up to date its various sections are, but it is definitely well worth bookmarking given the sheer number and classification of links.

Psychology in Bangor
http://www.psych.bangor.ac.uk/
This is the web site of the School of Psychology at the University of
Wales Bangor. You can send an email request for a prospectus, or for
information about applying for a place on its psychology degree
programme.

Psychology Lecture Notes Online
http://members.aol.com/nick8651/resources.htm
Produced by Nick Shackleton-Jones, lecturer in Psychology at
Yeovil College, these very useful resources are aimed at British A
level and first year degree psychology students. The free notes are
condensed, structured, and syllabus-specific. Teachers and lecturers
may also find them useful.

Psychology Virtual Library
http://www.clas.ufl.edu/users/gthursby/psi/
The Psychology Virtual Library keeps track of online information as
part of the World Wide Web Virtual Library. Sites are inspected
and evaluated for their adequacy as information sources before they
are linked from here. Well worth a look.

Social Psychology Network
http://www.wesleyan.edu/spn/
Social Psychology Network claims to be the largest social
psychology database on the internet. In these pages, you'll find a
staggering 4,000 links to psychology-related resources. Definitely
worth adding to your psychology bookmarks.

Society for Personality and Social Psychology
http://www.spsp.org/
With over 2,800 members, the Society claims to be the largest such
organisation of social and personality psychologists in the world. It
was founded in 1974 as Division 8 of the American Psychological
Association.

Society for the Quantitative Analyses of Behavior
http://www.jsu.edu/psychology/sqab.html

SQAB was founded in the USA in 1978 to present symposia and publish material which bring a quantitative analysis to bear on the understanding of behaviour.

University of the Philippines Psychology Society
http://psychsoc.org
Aside from content of local student interest, this useful site provides web links to psychology organisations and psychology resource pages worldwide.

Yahoo! – Branches of Psychology
http://www.yahoo.co.uk/Social_Science/Psychology/Branches/
..and finally, don't forget to make use of Yahoo!'s excellent and increasingly vast structured collection of online resources.

Bibliography

Aitchison, J. (1983) *The articulate mammal* (2nd ed.) London: Hutchinson.

Allport, D. A., Antonis, B. and Reynolds, P. (1972) On the division of attention: a disproof of the single channel hypothesis, *Quarterly Journal of Experimental Psychology* 24: 225–35.

Allport, D. A. (1980) Attention and performance: in G. Claxton *Cognitive psychology: New directions*. London: Routledge, Kegan Paul.

Allport, G. W.(1955) *Becoming – basic considerations for a psychology of personality*. New Haven, Connecticut: Yale University Press.

Anand, B. K. and Brobeck, J. R. (1951) Hypothalamic control of food intake in rats and cats. *Yale Journal of Biological Medicine* 24: 132–4.

Anderson, J. R. (1995) *Learning and memory: An integrated approach*. New York: John Wiley & Sons.

Argyle, M. and Crossland, J. (1987) The dimensions of positive emotions, *British Journal of Social Psychology* 26: 127–37.

Aronfreed, J. (1963) The effects of experimental socialization paradigms upon two moral responses to transgression. *Journal of Abnormal & Social Psychology* 66, 437–8.

Atkinson, R. C. and Shiffirin, R. M. (1971) The control of short-term memory. *Scentific American* 224: 82–90.

Ax, A. F. (1953) The physiological differentiation between fear and anger in humans. *Psychosomatic Medicine* 15: 433–42.

Ayllon, J. and Azrin, N. H. (1968) *The token economy*. New York: Appleton-Century-Crofts.

Baddeley, A. (1996) *Your Memory*, London: Prion.

Baddeley, A. D. (1995) Memory: in C. C. French and A. M. Coleman (eds.) *Cognitive Psychology*, London: Longman.

Baddeley, A. D. and Hitch, G. (1974) Working memory: in G. A. Bower (ed.) *Recent advances in learning and motivation*, Vol. 8, New

York: Academic Press.

Baddeley, A. D. *et al.* (1975) Imagery and visual working memory: in P. M. Rabbitt and S. Dornic (eds.) *Attention and performance,* Vol. V, London: Academic Press.

Baddeley, A. D. (1966) The influence of acoustic and sematic similarity on long term memory for word sequences. *Quarterly Journal of Experimental Psychology* 18: 302–9.

Baddeley, A. D. (1986) *Working memory.* Oxford: Oxford University Press.

Baddeley, A. D. (1990) *Human memory.* Hove, East Sussex: Lawrence Erlbaum Associates Ltd.

Bandura, A. and Walters, R. (1959) *Social learning and personality development.* New York: Holt.

Bandura, A. (1969) *Principles of behaviour modification,* New York: Reinhart and Winston.

Bandura, A. (1972) The stormy decade: fact or fiction? in D. Rogers (ed.) *Issues in adolescent psychology,* 2nd edn. New York: Appleton-Century.

Bandura, A., Ross, D. and Ross, S. A. (1961) Transmission of aggression through imitation of aggressive models. *Journal of Abnormal & Social Psychology* 63: 575–82.

Barrett, M. D. (1986) Early semantic representations and early word usage: in S. A. Kuczaj and M. D. Barrett (eds.) *The development of word meaning.* New York: Springer Verlag.

Bartlett, F. C. (1932) *Remembering.* Cambridge: Cambridge University Press.

Bates, E., Benignik L., Bretherton, I., Camaioni, L. and Velterra, V. (1979) *The emergence of symbols: Cognition and communication in infancy.* New York: Academic Press.

Bem, D. J. (1972) Self-perception theory: in L. Berkowitz (ed.) *Advances in experimental social psychology,* Vol. 6. New York: Academic Press.

Benton, D. (1981) ECT. *Can the system take the shock?* Community Care, 12 March, 15–17.

Bexton, W. H., Heron, W. and Scott, T. H. (1954) Effects of decreased variation in the sensory environment. *Canadian Journal of Psychology* 8, 70.

Biederman, I. (1987) Recognition-by-components: A theory of human image understanding. *Psychological Review* 94: 115–47.

Blakemore, C. (1988) *The mind machine,* London: BBC Publications.

Blos, P. (1967) The second individuation process of adolescence. *The psychoanalytic study of the child*, Vol. 22. New York: International University Press.

Borke, H. (1975) Piaget's mountains revisited: Changes in the egocentric landscape, *Developmental Psychology* 11: 240–3.

Botwinick, J. (1978) *Aging and behaviour* (2nd ed.). New York: Springer.

Bower, T. G. R. (1977) *The Perceptual World of the Child*. London: Fontana Paperbacks.

Bransford, J. D., Franks, J. J., Morris, C. D. and Stein, B. S. (1979) Some general constraints on learning and memory research: in L. S. Cerack and F. I. M. Craik (eds.) *Levels of processing in human memory*. New Jersey: Lawrence Erlbaum Associates Inc.

Brehm, J. W. (1966) *Theory of psychological reactance*. New York: Academic Press.

Broadbent, D. E. (1958) *Perception and communication*. London: Pergamon.

Brown, R. (1965) *Social psychology*. New York: Free Press.

Brown, R. and Kulick, J. (1977) Flashbulb memories. *Cognition* 5: 73–99.

Brown, R., Caden, C. B. and Bellugi, U. (1969) The child's grammar from 1 to 3: in J. P. Hill (ed.) *Minnesota Symposium on Child Psychology*, Vol. 2. Minneapolis: University of Minnesota Press.

Bruner, J. S. and Postman, L. (1949) On the perception of incongruity: A paradigm. *Journal of Personality* 18: 206–23.

Bruner, J. S. (1966) On the conservation of liquids: in J. S. Bruner, R. R. Olver and P. M. Greenfield (eds.), *Studies in cognitive growth*. New York: Wiley.

Bruner, J. S. (1975) The ontogenesis of speech acts. *Journal of Child Language* 2: 1–12.

Brunswick, E. (1956) *Perception and the representative design of psychological experiments*. Berkeley, California: University of California Press.

Butler, R. A. (1954) Curiosity in monkeys. *Scientific American*, February, 70–5.

Cannon, W. B. (1927) The James-Lang theory of emotions: A critical examination and an alternative. *American Journal of Psychology* 39: 106–24.

Carlson, N. R. (1992) *Foundations of Physiological Psychology* (2nd ed.).

Boston: Allyn & Bacon.

Cherry, E. C. (1953) Some experiments on the recognition of speech with one and two ears. *Journal of the Acoustical Society of America* 25: 975–9.

Chomsky, N. (1957) *Syntactic structures.* The Hague: Mounton.

Cohen, N. J. and Squire, L. R. (1980) Preserved learning and retention of pattern – analysing skills in amnesia: Dissociation of knowing how from knowing that, *Science* 210: 207–10.

Cohen, A. (1993) Everyday memory and memory systems, the experimental approach: in G. Cohen, G. Kiss and M. Le Voi, *Memory – current issues* (2nd edn.). Buckingham: Open University Press.

Cohen, G. (1986) Everyday memory: in G. Cohen, M. W. Eysenck and M.E. Le Voi (eds.) *Memory: A cognitive approach.* Milton Keynes: Open University Press.

Coleman, J. C. and Hendry, L. (1990) *The nature of adolescence* (2nd edn.) London: Routledge.

Collins. A. M. and Loftus, E. F. (1975) A spreading-activation theory of semantic processing. *Psychological Review* 82: 407–28.

Coon, D. (1993) *Introduction to Psychology* (3rd ed.). St Paul, Minnesota: West Publishing Co.

Craik, F. and Lockhart, R. (1972) Levels of processing. *Journal of Verbal Learning and Verbal Behaviour* 11: 671–84.

Cromer, R. F. (1974) The development of language and cognition: The cognition hypothesis: in B. Foss (ed.) *New perspectives in child development,* Harmondsworth, Middlesex: Penguin.

Cumming, E. and Henry, W. E. (1961) *Growing old: The process of disengagement.* New York: Basic Books.

Danziger, K. (1971) *Socialization.* Harmondsworth, Middlesex: Penguin.

Darley, J. M. and Latane, B. (1968) Bystander intervention in emergencies: Diffusion of responsibility. *Journal of Personality and Social Psychology* 8: 377–83.

Deregowski, J. (1972) Pictorial perception and culture. *Scientific American* 227: 82–8.

Deutsch, J. A. and Deutsch, D. (1963) Attention: Some theoretical considerations. *Psychological Review* 70: 80–90.

Donaldson, M. and McGarrigle, J. (1974) Some clues to the nature of semantic development. *Journal of Child Language* 1: 185–94.

Dowd, J. J. (1975) Ageing as exchange: A preface to theory. *Journal of Gerontology* 30: 584–94.

Dutton, D. C. and Aron, A. P. (1974) Some evidence for heightened sexual attraction under conditions of high anxiety. *Journal of Personality and Social Psychology* 30: 510–17.

Ekman, P. and Friesen, W. V. (1975) *Unmasking the face.* Englewood Cliffs, NJ: Prentice-Hall.

Ekman, P., Levenson, R. W. and Frieson, W. V. (1983) Autonomic nervous system activity distinguishing among emotions, *Science* 221: 1208–10.

Ekman, P. Friesen, W. V. and Ellsworth, P. (1972) *Emotion in the human face: Guidelines for research and an integration of findings.* New York: Pergamon.

Elkind, D. (1970) Erik Erikson's eight ages of man. *New York Times Magazine*, April 5.

Ellis, A. (1973) *Humanistic psychotherapy.* New York: McGraw Hill.

Engel, G. (1962) *Psychological development in health and disease.* Philadelphia: Saunders.

Erikson, E. H. (1968) *Identity: Youth and crisis.* New York: Norton.

Erikson, E. H. (1980) *Identity and the life cycle.* New York: Norton.

Eysenck, J. H. (1979) *The structure and measurement of intelligence.* New York: Springer.

Eysenck, M. W. and Keane, M. J. (1990) *Cognitive psychology: A Student's Handbook* (2nd edn 1995). Hove, East Sussex: Lawrence Erlbaum Associates Ltd.

Eysenck, M. W. (1984) *A handbook of cognitive psychology.* London: Lawrence Erlbaum Associates Ltd.

Eysenck, M. W. (1986) Working memory: in G. Cohen, M. W. Eysenck and M. A. Le Voi, *Memory: A cognitive approach.* Milton Keynes; Open University Press.

Festinger, L. (1957) *A theory of cognitive dissonance.* New York: Harper & Row.

Freud, S. (1976) *Psychopathology of everyday life*, Harmondsworth: Pelican.

Gardner, R. A. and Gardner, B. T. (1969) Teaching sign language to a chimpanzee. *Science* 165 (3894), 664–72.

Gibson, J. J. (1950) *The perception of the visual world.* Boston.

Houghton Mifflin.

Gibson, J. J. (1966) *The senses considered as perceptual systems*. Boston: Houghton Main.

Gibson, J. J. (1979) *The ecological approach to visual perception*. Boston: Houghton Mifflin.

Ginsburg, H. P. (1981) Piaget and education: The contributions and limits of genetic epistemology: in K. Richardson and S. Sheldon (eds.), *Cognitive development to adolescence*. Hove: Lawrence Erlbaum.

Glueck, S. and Glueck, E. T. (1950) Unravelling juvenile delinquency. *New York: Commomwealth Fund.*

Goffman, E. (1971) *The presentation of self in everyday life*. Harmondsworth, Middlesex: Penguin.

Gordon, E.(1989) *Theories of visual perception*, Chichester: Wiley.

Gould, R. L. (1978) *Transformations: Growth and change in adult life*. New York: Simon & Schuster.

Gregory, R. L. (1966) *Eye and Brain*, London: Weidenfeld & Nicolson.

Gregory, R. L. (1983) Visual illusions: in J. Miller (ed.) *States of mind*. London: BBC Publications.

Guilford, J. P. (1967) *The nature of human intelligence*. New York: McGraw Hill.

Hall, G. S. (1904) *Adolescence*. New York; Appleton & Co.

Hartshorne, H. and May, M. (1930) *Studies in the nature of character*. New York: Macmillan.

Havinghurst, R. J. (1964) Stages of vocational development: in H. Borow (ed.) *Man in a world of work*. Boston: Houghton Mifflin.

Hebb, D. O. (1949) *The organisation of behaviour*, New York: Wiley.

Heron, E. (1957) The pathology of boredom. *Scientific American* 196: 52–69.

Hocket, C. D. (1960) The origins of speech. *Scientific American* 203: 88–89.

Hoffman, M. L. (1970) Conscience personality and socialization techniques. *Human Development* 13: 90–126.

Hoffman, M. L. (1976) Empathy, role taking, guilt and development of altruistic motives: in T. Lickona (ed.) *Moral development and behaviour*. New York: Holt, Rhinehart & Winston.

Horn, J. L. and Cattell, R. B. (1967) Age differences in fluid and crystallized intelligence. *Acta Psychologica* 26: 107–29.

Howes, D. and Solomon, R. L. (1950) A note on McGinnies' emotionality and perceptual defence. *Psychological Review* 57: 229–34.

Hubel D. H. and Wiesal, T. N. (1968) Receptive fields and functional architecture of monkey striate cortex, *Journal of Physiology*, 59.

Hubel, D. H. and Wiesel, T. N. (1959) Receptive fields of single neurons in the cat's striate cortex. *Journal of Physiology* 148: 579–91.

Hull, C. L. (1943) *Principles of Behaviour*. New York: Appleton, Century Crofts.

James, W. (1890) *Principles of psychology*. New York: Holt.

Kahnemann, D. (1973) *Attention and effort*. Englewood Cliffs, New Jersey: Prentice Hall.

Kalish, R.A. (1982) *Late adulthood: Perspectives on human development* (2nd ed.). Monterey, CA: Brooks/Cole.

Kelvin, P. (1981) Work as a source of identity: The implications of unemployment. *British Journal of Guidance and Counselling*, 9 (1) 2–11.

Kandel, E. R., Schwartz, J. H., Jessell, T. M. (1991) *Principles of neural science* (3rd ed.) Connecticut: Prentice Hall.

Kleinmuntz, B. (1980) *Essentials of abnormal psychology* (2nd ed.). London: Harper & Row.

Kohlberg, L. (1969) Stage and sequence: The cognitive developmental approach to socialization: in D. A. Goslin (ed.) *Handbook of socialization theory and research*. Chicago: Rand McNally.

Laing, R. D. (1967) *The politics of experience and the bird of paradise*, Harmondsworth, Middlesex: Penguin.

Lashley, K. (1929) *Brain mechanisms and intelligence: A quantitative study of injuries to the brain*. Chicago, Illinois: University of Chicago Press.

Latane, B. and Rodin, J. (1969) A lady in distress: Inhibiting effects of friends and strangers on bystander intervention. *Journal of Experimental Social Psychology* 5: 189–202.

Lazarus, A. A. (1976) *Multimodal behaiour therapy*. New York: Springer.

Lenneberg, E. H. (1967) *Biological foundations of language*. New York:

Wiley.

Lepper, M. R. and Greene, D. (1978) Overjustification research and beyond: Towards a means-end analysis of intrinsic and extrinsic motivation: in M. R Lepper and D. Greene (eds.) *The hidden costs of reward*. Hillsdale, New Jersey: Lawrence Erlbaum Associates Inc.

Levinson, D. J., Darrow, D. N., Klein, E. B., Levinson, M. H. and Mckee, B. (1978) *The seasons of man's life*. New York: A. A. Knopf.

Loftus, E. F. and Palmer, J. C. (1974) Reconstruction of automobile destruction: An example of the interaction between language and memory. *Journal of Verbal Learning and Verbal Behaviour* 13: 585–9.

Loftus, E. F. and Zanni, G. (1975) Eyewitness testimony: The influence of the wording of a question. *Bulletin of the Psychonomic Society* 5: 86–8.

Logan, G. D. (1988) Toward an instance theory of automisation. *Psychological Review* 95: 492–527.

Maddox, G. L. (1964) Disengagement theory. A critical evaluation. *The Gerontologist* 4: 80–3.

Marr, D. (1982) *Vision: A computational investigation into the human representation of visual information*. San Francisco: W. H. Freeman.

Maslow, A. (1954) *Motivation and personality*. New York: Harper & Row.

Mayer, J. (1955) Regulation of energy intake and the body weight The glucostatic theory and the Lipostatic hypothesis. *Annals of the New York Academy of Sciences* 63: 15–43.

McGinnies, E. (1949) Emotionality and perceptual defense *Psychological Review* 56: 244–51.

McClelland, D. C., Atkinson, J., Clark, R. and Lowell, E. (1953) *The achievement motive*. New York: Appleton-Century-Croft.

Minsky, M. (1975) A framework for representing knowledge: in P H. Winston (ed.) *The psychology of computer vision*. New York McGraw Hill.

Murray, H.A. (ed.) (1938) *Explorations in personality*. New York Oxford University Press.

Neisser, U. (1964) Visual search. *Scientific American* 210: 94–102.

Neisser, U. (1976) *Cognition and reality*. San Francisco: W. H Freeman.

Nelson, K. (1973) Structure and strategy in learning to talk

Monographs of the Society for Research in Child Development 38: 149.

Nesselroade, J. R., Schaie, K. W. and Batter, P. B. (1972) Ontogenetic and generational components of structual and quantitative change in adult behaviour. *Journal of Gerontology* 27: 222–8.

Norman, D. A. and Shallice, T. (1980) *Attention to action: Willed and automatic control of behaviour (CHIP Report 99)*. San Diego, California: University of California.

Offer, D. (1969) *The psychological world of the teenager*, New York: Basic Books.

Olds, J. and Milner, P. (1954) Positive reinforcement produced by electrical stimulation of septal area and other regions of the rat brain. *Journal of Comparative and Physiological Psychology* 47: 419–27.

Osgood, C. E. (1966) Dimensionality of the semantic space for communication via facial expression, *Scandinavian Journal of Psychology* 7: 1–3.

Paivio, A. (1986) *Mental representations: A dual coding approach.* Oxford: Oxford University Press.

Parke, R. D. (1972) Some effects of punishment on children's behaviour: in W. W. Harting (ed.) *The young child*, Vol. 2. Washington DC: National Association for the Education of Young Children.

Parke, R. D. (1974) Rules, roles and resistance to deviation: Recent advances in punishment, descipline and self control: in A. D. Pick (ed.) *Minnesota Symposium on Child Psychology*, Vol. 8. Minneapolis, Minnesota: University of Minnesota Press.

Parke, R. D. (1977) Some effects of punishment on children's behaviour revisited. In Hetherington, E. M., and Parke, R. D. (eds.) *Contemporary readings in child psychology.* New York: McGraw Hill.

Patterson, F. G. (1980) Innovative uses of language by a gorilla: A case study: in K. Nelson (ed.) *Children's language*, Vol. 2. New York: Gardner Press.

Perry, D. G. and Parke, R. D. (1975) Punishment and alternative response training as determinants of response inhibition in children. *Genetic Psychology Monographs* 91: 257–79.

Piaget, J. and Inhelder, B. (1969) *The psychology of the child*, New York: Basic Books.

Piaget, J. (1973) *The Child's Conception of the World.* London:

Paladin.

Piliavin, I. M., Rodin, J. and Piliavin, J. A. (1969) Good samaritanism: An underground phenomenon? *Journal of Personality and Social Psychology* 13: 289–99.

Piliavin, J. A., Dovidio, J. F., Gaertner, S. L. and Clark, R. D. (1981) *Emergency intervention*. New York: Academic Press.

Pinel, J. P. J. (1993) *Biopsychology* (2nd edn.). Boston: Allyn & Bacon.

Plutchik, R. (1980) *Emotion: A psychobioevolutionary synthesis*. New York: Harper & Row.

Rabbitt, P. M. A. (1967) Ignoring irrelevant information. *American Journal of Psychology* 80: 1–13.

Richmond, P. G. (1970) *An introduction to Piaget*. London: Routledge & Kegan Paul.

Rolls, E. T. and Rolls, B. J. (1982) Brain mechanisms involved in feeding: in L. M. Barker (ed.) *The psychobiology of human food selection*. Westport, CT: AVI Publishing Company.

Rubin, Z. and McNeil, E. B. (1983) *The psychology of being human* (3rd edn.). London: Harper & Row.

Rumelhart, D. E. and Norman, D. A. (1985) Representations of knowledge: in M. M. Aitkenhead and J. M. Slack (eds.) *Issues in cognitive modelling*, London: Lawrence Erlbaum.

Rutter, M., Graham, P., Chadwick, D. F. D. and Yule, W. (1976) Adolescent turmoil: Fact or fiction. *Journal of Child Psychology and Psychiatry* 17: 35–56.

Salame, P. and Baddeley, A. D. (1982) Disruption of short-term memory by unattended speech: implications for the structure of working memory. *Journal of Verbal Learning and Verbal Behaviour* 21: 150–64.

Savage Rumbaugh *et al.* (1980) The linguistic essential, *Science* 210: 922–5.

Schachter, S. and Singer, J. E. (1962) Cognitive, social and physiological determinants of emotional state. *Psychological Review* 69: 379–99.

Schachter, S. and Wheeler, L. (1962) Epinephrine, Chlorpromazine and amusement, *Journal of Abnormal and Social Psychology* 65: 121–8.

Schachter, S. (1964) The interaction of cognitive and psysiological determinants of emotional state: in L. Berkowitz (ed.) *Advances in experimental social psychology*, Vol. 1. New York: Academic Press.

Schlosberg, H. S. (1941) A scale for the judgement of facial expression. *Journal of Experimental Psychology* 29: 497–510.

Schneider, K. (1959) Primary and secondary symptoms in schizophrenia: in R. R. Hirsch and M. Shepherd (eds.) (1974) *Themes and variations in European psychiatry.* New York: John Wright.

Sears, R. R., Maccoby, E. and Levin, H. (1957) *Patterns of child rearing.* Evanston, Illinois: Row, Petersen and Co.

Shallice, T. (1982) Specific impairments of planning. *Philosophical Transactions of the Royal Society of London* 13298: 199–209.

Sherrington, C. S. (1900) Experiments on the value of vascular and visceral factors for the geneses of emotion. *Proceedings of the Royal Society* 66: 390–403.

Siddique, C. M. and D'Arcy, C. (1984) Adolescence, stress and psychological well-being. *Journal of Youth and Adolescence* 13: 459–74.

Simmons, R. and Rosenberg, S. (1975) Sex, sex roles and self-image. *Journal of Youth and Adolescence* 4: 229–56.

Skinner, B. F. (1957) *Verbal behavior.* New York: Appleton-Century-Crofts.

Slater, A., Slater, E. and Roth, M. (1969) *Clinical psychiatry* (3rd ed.). London: Balliere, Tindall and Cassell.

Slobin, D. I. (1975) On the nature of talk to children: in E. H. Lenneberg and E. Lenneberg (eds.) *Foundation of Language Development*, Vol. 1. New York: Academic Press.

Snow, C. E. (1977) Mother's speech research: From input to interaction: in C. E. Snow and C. A. Ferguson (eds.) *Talking to children: Language input and acquisition.* New York: Cambridge University Press.

Solso, R. (1995) *Cognitive Psycholgy* (4th edn.) Boston: Allyn and Bacon.

Spearman, C. (1967) The doctrine of two factors: in S. Wiseman (ed.) *Intelligence and ability.* Harmondsworth: Penguin.

Speisman, J. C., Lazarus, R. S., Mordkoff, A. M. and Davidson, L. A. (1964) The experimental reduction of stress based on ego defense theory. *Journal of Abnormal and Social Psychology* 68: 397–8.

Spitzer, R. L., Endicott, J. and Robins, E. (1978) Research

diagnostic criteria: Rationale and reliability. *Archives of General Psychiatry* 35: 773–82.

Sternberg, R. J. (1984) Towards a triarchic theory of human intelligence. *The Behavioral and Brain Sciences* 7: 269–315.

Taylor, J. (1992) A questionable treatment. *Nursing Times* 88 (40): 41–3.

Teitelbaum, P. and Stellar, E. (1954) Recovery from the failure to eat produced by hypothalamic lesions. *Science* 120: 894–5.

Teitelbaum, P. (1967) Motivation and control of food intake: in C. F. Code (ed.), *Handbook of physiology: Alimentary canal*, Vol. 1. Washington, DC: American Physiological Society.

Thigpen, C. H. and Cleckley, H. (1954) A case of multiple personality. *Journal of Abnormal and Social Psychology* 49: 135–51.

Thurstone, L. L. (1938) Primary mental abilities: in *Psychometric Monographs*, No. 1.

Treisman, A. M. and Geffen, G. (1967) Selective attention: perception, or response? *Quarterly Journal of Experimental Psychology* 19: 1–18.

Treisman, A. M (1964) Verbal cues, language and meaning in selective attention. *American Journal of Psychology* 77: 206–19.

Tulvin, E. *et al.* (1974) Cue dependent forgetting, *American Scientist* 62: 74–82.

Tulvin, E. (1985) How many memory systems are there? *American Psychologist* 40: 385–98.

Tulvin, E. (1972) Episodic and sematic memory: in E. Tulvin and W. Donaldson (eds.), *Organization of memory*. London: Academic Press.

Underwood, B.J. (1957) Interference and forgetting. *Psychological Review* 64: 49–60.

Vernon, P. E. (1971) *The structure of human abilities*. London: Academic Press.

Vernon, M.D. (1955) The functions of schemata in perceiving. *Psychological Review* 62: 180–92.

Vygotsky, L.S. (1978) *Mind in society*. Cambridge, Massachusetts: Harvard University Press.

Wickens, (1984) Processing resources in attention: in R. Parasuraman and D. R. Davies (eds.) Varieties of attention, London: Academic Press.

Wolpe, J. (1978) Cognition and causation in human behaviour and its therapy. *American Psychologist* 33: 437–46.

Index

HOW TO STUDY AND LEARN
Your practical guide to effective study skills
Dr Peter Marshall

Are you thinking of studying or training for an important qualification? Do you know the best techniques for studying and learning to ensure you achieve the best results as quickly as possible? Whether you are at college or university, doing projects or assignments, writing essays, receiving continuous assessment or preparing for exams this is the book for you. Now in its third edition, this practical book covers getting your thinking right, organising yourself properly, finding and processing the information you need, reading effectively, developing good writing skills, thinking creatively, motivating yourself, and more. Whatever your subject, age or background, start now and turn yourself into a winning candidate.

UNLOCKING YOUR POTENTIAL
How to master your mind, life and destiny
Dr Peter Marshall

If you really want to unlock your potential and become master of your own life, you will need to remove the barriers to success, including your own narrow expectations and those imposed by others. This book will introduce you to techniques for overcoming the limiting effects of past conditioning, misguided or obsolete teachings and repressed conflicts. You will learn how to develop your creativity, improve your ability to solve problems and manage your social contacts to facilitate success.

MAXIMISING YOUR MEMORY
How to train yourself to remember more
Dr Peter Marshall

A powerful memory brings obvious advantages in educational, career and social terms. At school and college those certificates that provide a passport to a career depend heavily on what you can remember in the exam room. In the world of work, being able to recall details which slip the minds of colleagues will give you a competitive edge. In addition, one of the secrets of being popular with customers and friends is to remember their names and the little things that make them feel they matter to you. This popular book, now in its second edition, explains clearly how you can maximise your memory in order to achieve your academic, professional and personal goals.

UNDERSTANDING HUMAN MEMORY
What it is and how it Works
Dr Peter Marshall

This book explores the subject of human memory in all its dimensions – how it works physiologically and chemically, how it develops by conditioning and training, how it sometimes plays tricks on us to protect us, how it can fail through physiological damage and what we can do if it does. Now in its second edition, it will be essential reading for students of psychology, nursing, medicine and other disciplines concerned with understanding and management of human behaviour.

RESEARCH METHODS
How to choose and use the right methods
Dr Peter Marshall

All social science courses offered at universities or colleges include a research methods module, for which students are expected to purchase a research methods book. These are invariably weighty and expensive at a time when student funds are stretched. Dr Marshall has produced a reader-friendly, plain English and value-for-money solution. In this second edition, he explains the various methods available to social researchers and the basic principles, strengths and weakness involved in the use of both quantitative and qualitative methods. Whether you are new to the subject or an established practitioner this book should prove valuable. Dr Marshall has had many years experience in research and teaching in universities and colleges

IMPROVING YOUR MEMORY
The unique 5 x 5 system
Dr Peter Marshall

In the 21st century people live on their wits. What determines how successful they are in whatever they do is their mental ability and, to a large extent, that depends on their memory quality. The author and colleagues of London University discovered that memory quality has even replaced IQ as the dominant predictor of school outcomes. Deriving from such research, this book, now in its third edition, contains a powerful system for enhancing memory quality. Written in plain, concise language, it is simple, effective and comprehensive in its application. It has been tested over and over again on the young, the old, the bright and the not so bright and it can be mastered in just 7 – 10 hours.

A HANDBOOK OF HYPNOTHERAPY
A practitioner's guide
Dr Peter Marshall

In simple, plain English style, this book will guide you through the entire subject – the theories underlying hypnosis, the disorders it can be used to treat, the wide range of procedures and the protocols for treating different conditions. You will find step-by-step guidance on how to conduct a course of hypnotherapy, from the initial consultation, through establishing rapport with the client, taking a case history, deciding on the appropriate techniques to use, setting realistic therapy aims and objectives, psycho-education, gathering of therapy resources, induction, deepening, therapeutic intervention, ego strengthening to wakening the patient. There is even a chapter that deals with all aspects of managing a successful therapy practice.

EDUCATING A GIFTED CHILD
A guide for parents and teachers
Dr Peter Marshall

It is generally accepted today, and also UK government policy, that educational authorities must make provision for meeting the needs of gifted children. But how should they go about it? There is so much lack of agreement about what is the best strategy, about how to identify the gifted youngsters and even about what the concept of giftedness means. The author is a leading expert, who holds a doctorate from Manchester University in this subject. In plain English, in a balanced way and in a logical order, he covers everything a teacher, or a parent needs to know to meet the challenge of educating a gifted child.